I0344005

Personal Information

Name: _____

Email: _____

Home: _____

Office: _____

Cell: _____

www.kaysupasaiyan.com

 Kayla Chew Enterprises LLC.

1. START WITH THE BIG PICTURE. BELIEVE IN THE PROCESS!

The first step in goal setting is having confidence in yourself and your abilities. Believe and trust in the process. Think about your bigger picture and the direction you want your life to go in. Dream BIG and Dream BETTER!

2. WRITE IT DOWN . SET YOUR GOALS!

Think about the different areas in your life you'd like to change or improve. Write your goals down and schedule dates for their completion. Break down your goals into steps. Plan your steps wisely, establishing a realistic time frame that will allow you to carry out those steps.

3. BE CONSISTENT. REMAIN ACCOUNTABLE

Review your goals throughout the year, weekly, or monthly . Any way that works for you. Be consistent, make sure you're on course and make sure to celebrate your milestones. Remain accountable in your everyday life. Things will get hard, days will be tough. Think about your bigger picture. Never forget that you can do anything you put your mind to.

4. DON'T BE AFRAID TO ASK FOR HELP. DELEGATE!

Ask for help and learn from those around you. Hire an assistant, ask a professional for advice. Get a mentor! Never stop learning and don't be afraid to get help if you find yourself overwhelmed or stuck.

5. ASSESS YOUR PROGRESS. STAY ON COURSE.

Continue to assess your progress and review your goals. Our goals are constantly changing and evolving. Learn from your mistakes and continue to grow.

BE A GOAL CRUSHER!

WWW.KAYSUPASAIYAN.COM

2021 Calendar

January
S	M	T	W	T	F	S
					1	2
3	4	5	6	7	8	9
10	11	12	13	14	15	16
17	18	19	20	21	22	23
24	25	26	27	28	29	30
31						

February
S	M	T	W	T	F	S
	1	2	3	4	5	6
7	8	9	10	11	12	13
14	15	16	17	18	19	20
21	22	23	24	25	26	27
28						

March
S	M	T	W	T	F	S
	1	2	3	4	5	6
7	8	9	10	11	12	13
14	15	16	17	18	19	20
21	22	23	24	25	26	27
28	29	30	31			

April
S	M	T	W	T	F	S
				1	2	3
4	5	6	7	8	9	10
11	12	13	14	15	16	17
18	19	20	21	22	23	24
25	26	27	28	29	30	

May
S	M	T	W	T	F	S
						1
2	3	4	5	6	7	8
9	10	11	12	13	14	15
16	17	18	19	20	21	22
23	24	25	26	27	28	29
30	31					

June
S	M	T	W	T	F	S
		1	2	3	4	5
6	7	8	9	10	11	12
13	14	15	16	17	18	19
20	21	22	23	24	25	26
27	28	29	30			

July
S	M	T	W	T	F	S
				1	2	3
4	5	6	7	8	9	10
11	12	13	14	15	16	17
18	19	20	21	22	23	24
25	26	27	28	29	30	31

August
S	M	T	W	T	F	S
1	2	3	4	5	6	7
8	9	10	11	12	13	14
15	16	17	18	19	20	21
22	23	24	25	26	27	28
29	30	31				

September
S	M	T	W	T	F	S
			1	2	3	4
5	6	7	8	9	10	11
12	13	14	15	16	17	18
19	20	21	22	23	24	25
26	27	28	29	30		

October
S	M	T	W	T	F	S
					1	2
3	4	5	6	7	8	9
10	11	12	13	14	15	16
17	18	19	20	21	22	23
24	25	26	27	28	29	30
31						

November
S	M	T	W	T	F	S
	1	2	3	4	5	6
7	8	9	10	11	12	13
14	15	16	17	18	19	20
21	22	23	24	25	26	27
28	29	30				

December
S	M	T	W	T	F	S
			1	2	3	4
5	6	7	8	9	10	11
12	13	14	15	16	17	18
19	20	21	22	23	24	25
26	27	28	29	30	31	

2022 Calendar

January
S	M	T	W	T	F	S
						1
2	3	4	5	6	7	8
9	10	11	12	13	14	15
16	17	18	19	20	21	22
23	24	25	26	27	28	29
30	31					

February
S	M	T	W	T	F	S
		1	2	3	4	5
6	7	8	9	10	11	12
13	14	15	16	17	18	19
20	21	22	23	24	25	26
27	28					

March
S	M	T	W	T	F	S
		1	2	3	4	5
6	7	8	9	10	11	12
13	14	15	16	17	18	19
20	21	22	23	24	25	26
27	28	29	30	31		

April
S	M	T	W	T	F	S
					1	2
3	4	5	6	7	8	9
10	11	12	13	14	15	16
17	18	19	20	21	22	23
24	25	26	27	28	29	30

May
S	M	T	W	T	F	S
1	2	3	4	5	6	7
8	9	10	11	12	13	14
15	16	17	18	19	20	21
22	23	24	25	26	27	28
29	30	31				

June
S	M	T	W	T	F	S
			1	2	3	4
5	6	7	8	9	10	11
12	13	14	15	16	17	18
19	20	21	22	23	24	25
26	27	28	29	30		

July
S	M	T	W	T	F	S
					1	2
3	4	5	6	7	8	9
10	11	12	13	14	15	16
17	18	19	20	21	22	23
24	25	26	27	28	29	30
31						

August
S	M	T	W	T	F	S
	1	2	3	4	5	6
7	8	9	10	11	12	13
14	15	16	17	18	19	20
21	22	23	24	25	26	27
28	29	30	31			

September
S	M	T	W	T	F	S
				1	2	3
4	5	6	7	8	9	10
11	12	13	14	15	16	17
18	19	20	21	22	23	24
25	26	27	28	29	30	

October
S	M	T	W	T	F	S
						1
2	3	4	5	6	7	8
9	10	11	12	13	14	15
16	17	18	19	20	21	22
23	24	25	26	27	28	29
30	31					

November
S	M	T	W	T	F	S
		1	2	3	4	5
6	7	8	9	10	11	12
13	14	15	16	17	18	19
20	21	22	23	24	25	26
27	28	29	30			

December
S	M	T	W	T	F	S
				1	2	3
4	5	6	7	8	9	10
11	12	13	14	15	16	17
18	19	20	21	22	23	24
25	26	27	28	29	30	31

BEGIN WITH *The End* IN MIND

Vision Board

About Me

What do I love most about my life?

What do I want more of in my life?

What does my dream life look like?

How do I define success? Why?

Where do I want to be in 5 or 10 years?

Is there anything I need to let go of (fears, pain)? If so, what would I do if I didn't have these fears?

About Me

What motivates me?

What obstacles are standing in my way or holding me back from accomplishing my goals?

How will accomplishing these goals improve my life?

How will I celebrate after accomplishing my goals?

MINDSET
is everything

Mindset

"What you think, you create. What you feel, you attract. What You imagine, you become"

What I've Attracted into my life:

What I want to attract into my life:

How can I change my mindset to attract what I want?

What I want to See Come Into My Life

PERSONAL GROWTH	RELATIONSHIPS	MENTAL HEALTH

SPIRITUAL GROWTH	PHYSICAL HEALTH	HOME

CAREER	FINANCE	TRAVEL

COMMUNITY	SUCCESS	ADVENTURE

Goal Planner

ATTRACT	BE	TREAT	DELEGATE	EXPLORE
TRAVEL TO	DO MORE	DO LESS	PRACTICE	BE OPEN TO
VISIT	READ	IMPROVE	ORGANIZE	CREATE
EXPERIENCE	LISTEN TO	LEARN TO	SIMPLIFY	START A
SUPPORT	WATCH	BELIEVE	MODIFY	INVENT A
TRY	SIGN UP FOR	ALLOW	ELIMINATE	LET GO OF
ATTEND	HELP	RECEIVE	REVISE	GIVE

My Goals

PERSONAL

PROFESSIONAL

NEW THINGS To Try

PEOPLE I WANT To See

PLACES I WANT To Visit

HOW CAN I Help Other People

RELATIONSHIPS

AFFIRMATION

TIME FRAME	GOAL	KEY STEPS
30 DAYS		
60 DAYS		
90 DAYS		
1 YEAR		
3 YEARS		
6 YEARS		
10 YEARS		

Key Monthly GOALS

MONTH	GOAL OF THE MONTH	ACHIEVED
1		
2		
3		
4		
5		
6		
7		
8		
9		
10		
11		
12		

Top Goals

What are the top 3 goals you wish to achieve this year?

1.

2.

3.

How will achieving these goals affect your life?

_____
_____
_____
_____
_____

25 Daily HABIT IDEAS

1. Create a morning & Nightly Routine
2. Wake up and go to bed early
3. Stretch as soon as you get out of bed.
4. Make your bed every morning
5. Morning & Evening Meditation & Reflection
6. 30 min - 1hr Workout
7. Make a Plan for your day
8. Dedicate time to learning: Books, Podcast, classes
9. List three things you are grateful for
10. Stay focused and keep your to-do list small
11. Set out your clothes for the next day
12. Laugh even if you have to force it
13. Get some sun and take a walk
14. Treat yourself to something
15. Adopt a productive hobby
16. Invest 30 minutes a day to a hobby you enjoy
17. Keep yourself informed about things going on in the world
18. Think of an affirmation and repeat it throughout the day
19. Review the day what worked? What didn't?
20. Make a list for tomorrow to clear your mind before you sleep
21. Practice to express your opinion without getting offended
22. Look for the positives in everything
23. Track your daily finances
24. Think about how you can learn from your mistakes
25. Take a break from social media

YOU ARE CAPABLE OF *Amazing Things!*

Top Goal

Write your number 1 goal in the circle. Brainstorm 4 action steps that will help you towards your goal.

It's important we remember to celebrate our achievements. Write down what you would do to celebrate the success of achieving this goal.

Why do I want to achieve this goal:

How will I feel when I've reached this goal:

What are my challenges/obstacles:

Free space for notes sketching, mind-mapping and more.

SET A GOAL MAKE A PLAN. YOUR POSSIBILITIES ARE LIMITLESS.

Vision is EVERYTHING

30 Day CHALLENGE

This month I will challenge myself by:

1	2	3	4	5	6	7	8	9	10
11	12	13	14	15	16	17	18	19	20
21	22	23	24	25	26	27	28	29	30

My reason why:

Action Steps:

- _____
- _____
- _____

- _____
- _____
- _____

I will celebrate by:

What is your number 1 goal for this month? Write it in the circle. Brainstorm 4 action steps that will help you towards your goal.

How will achieving this goal improve my life?

What is in my way? How can I make it go away?

ACTION STEPS

1
- _____
- _____
- _____
- _____

2
- _____
- _____
- _____
- _____

3
- _____
- _____
- _____
- _____

4
- _____
- _____
- _____
- _____

Time I am willing to set aside to complete my tasks: _____

Month:

SUNDAY	MONDAY	TUESDAY	WEDNESDAY	THURSDAY	FRIDAY	SATURDAY

GOALS

AFFIRMATION

PRIORITIES

NOTES

APPOINTMENTS	IMPORTANT DATES	BIRTHDAYS	SPECIAL EVENTS

THIS MONTH I WILL EXPAND MY KNOWLEDGE AND LEARN ABOUT

Monthly Book List

BOOK	BOOK	BOOK	BOOK
☆☆☆☆☆ ☐	☆☆☆☆☆ ☐	☆☆☆☆☆ ☐	☆☆☆☆☆ ☐
Progress	Progress	Progress	Progress

Identify the habits that you will practice daily to help you achieve your monthly goals.

HABIT TRACKER	1	2	3	4	5	6	7	8	9	10	11	12	13	14	15	16	17	18	19	20	21	22	23	24	25	26	27	28	29	30	31

Week:

MONDAY

TUESDAY

WEDNESDAY

THURSDAY

FRIDAY

SATURDAY

SUNDAY

PASSION. PURPOSE. PROGRESS. NEVER STOP GROWING!

This Week I am Grateful for:

TO DO:

- _____
- _____
- _____
- _____
- _____
- _____
- _____

- _____
- _____
- _____
- _____
- _____
- _____
- _____

- _____
- _____
- _____
- _____
- _____
- _____
- _____

APPOINTMENTS

- _____
- _____
- _____
- _____
- _____
- _____
- _____
- _____

MEALS

M _____
T _____
W _____
TH _____
F _____
S _____
SU _____

SHOPPING LIST

- _____
- _____
- _____
- _____
- _____
- _____
- _____
- _____

NOTES

Weekly Reflection

On a scale of 1-10, rate your week. - 1 2 3 4 5 6 7 8 9 10

How am I feeling? Why do I feel this way?

What went well this week? How am I progressing?

This week I learned:

I would like to improve on:

Things I am proud of?

Weekly Reflection

Things I need to let go of?

What habits did I maintain?

What habits were difficult for me to maintain?

How can I make next week better?

What will be realistic targets for next week? Do I need to revise my objectives

Week:

MONDAY

TUESDAY

WEDNESDAY

THURSDAY

FRIDAY

SATURDAY

SUNDAY

PASSION. PURPOSE. PROGRESS. NEVER STOP GROWING!

This Week I am Grateful for:

TO DO:

- _____
- _____
- _____
- _____
- _____
- _____
- _____

- _____
- _____
- _____
- _____
- _____
- _____
- _____

- _____
- _____
- _____
- _____
- _____
- _____
- _____

APPOINTMENTS

- _____
- _____
- _____
- _____
- _____
- _____
- _____
- _____

MEALS

M _____
T _____
W _____
TH _____
F _____
S _____
SU _____

SHOPPING LIST

- _____
- _____
- _____
- _____
- _____
- _____
- _____
- _____

NOTES

Weekly Reflection

On a scale of 1-10, rate your week. - 1 2 3 4 5 6 7 8 9 10

How am I feeling? Why do I feel this way?

What went well this week? How am I progressing?

This week I learned:

I would like to improve on:

Things I am proud of?

Weekly Reflection

Things I need to let go of?

What habits did I maintain?

What habits were difficult for me to maintain?

How can I make next week better?

What will be realistic targets for next week? Do I need to revise my objectives

Week:

MONDAY

TUESDAY

WEDNESDAY

THURSDAY

FRIDAY

SATURDAY

SUNDAY

PASSION. PURPOSE. PROGRESS. NEVER STOP GROWING!

This Week I am Grateful for:

TO DO:

- _____
- _____
- _____
- _____
- _____
- _____
- _____

- _____
- _____
- _____
- _____
- _____
- _____
- _____

- _____
- _____
- _____
- _____
- _____
- _____
- _____

APPOINTMENTS

- _____
- _____
- _____
- _____
- _____
- _____
- _____

MEALS

M _____
T _____
W _____
TH _____
F _____
S _____
SU _____

SHOPPING LIST

- _____
- _____
- _____
- _____
- _____
- _____
- _____

NOTES

Weekly Reflection

On a scale of 1-10, rate your week. - 1 2 3 4 5 6 7 8 9 10

How am I feeling? Why do I feel this way?

What went well this week? How am I progressing?

This week I learned:

I would like to improve on:

Things I am proud of?

Weekly Reflection

Things I need to let go of?

What habits did I maintain?

What habits were difficult for me to maintain?

How can I make next week better?

**What will be realistic targets for next week?
Do I need to revise my objectives**

Week:

MONDAY	TUESDAY	WEDNESDAY

THURSDAY	FRIDAY	SATURDAY

SUNDAY

PASSION. PURPOSE. PROGRESS. NEVER STOP GROWING!

This Week I am Grateful for:

TO DO:

- _____
- _____
- _____
- _____
- _____
- _____
- _____

- _____
- _____
- _____
- _____
- _____
- _____
- _____

- _____
- _____
- _____
- _____
- _____
- _____
- _____

APPOINTMENTS

- _____
- _____
- _____
- _____
- _____
- _____
- _____

MEALS

M _____
T _____
W _____
TH _____
F _____
S _____
SU _____

SHOPPING LIST

- _____
- _____
- _____
- _____
- _____
- _____
- _____

NOTES

Weekly Reflection

On a scale of 1-10, rate your week. - 1 2 3 4 5 6 7 8 9 10

How am I feeling? Why do I feel this way?

What went well this week? How am I progressing?

This week I learned:

I would like to improve on:

Things I am proud of?

Weekly Reflection

Things I need to let go of?

What habits did I maintain?

What habits were difficult for me to maintain?

How can I make next week better?

What will be realistic targets for next week? Do I need to revise my objectives

Week:

MONDAY

TUESDAY

WEDNESDAY

THURSDAY

FRIDAY

SATURDAY

SUNDAY

PASSION. PURPOSE. PROGRESS. NEVER STOP GROWING!

This Week I am Grateful for:

TO DO:

APPOINTMENTS

MEALS

M
T
W
TH
F
S
SU

SHOPPING LIST

NOTES

Weekly Reflection

On a scale of 1-10, rate your week. - 1 2 3 4 5 6 7 8 9 10

How am I feeling? Why do I feel this way?

What went well this week? How am I progressing?

This week I learned:

I would like to improve on:

Things I am proud of?

Weekly Reflection

Things I need to let go of?

What habits did I maintain?

What habits were difficult for me to maintain?

How can I make next week better?

**What will be realistic targets for next week?
Do I need to revise my objectives**

I *accomplish* ANYTHING I FOCUS ON

Monthly Reflection

What went well this month? How am I progressing?

Did I reach my goal? Why or why not?

How will I rate my efforts this month? How can I get better?

What will be realistic targets for next month? Do I need to revise my objectives?

Free space for notes sketching, mind-mapping and more.

SET A GOAL MAKE A PLAN. YOUR POSSIBILITIES ARE LIMITLESS.

Dream ENORMOUSLY *Big*

30 Day CHALLENGE

This month I will challenge myself by:

1	2	3	4	5	6	7	8	9	10
11	12	13	14	15	16	17	18	19	20
21	22	23	24	25	26	27	28	29	30

My reason why:

Action Steps:

- _____
- _____
- _____
- _____
- _____
- _____

I will celebrate by:

What is your number 1 goal for this month? Write it in the circle. Brainstorm 4 action steps that will help you towards your goal.

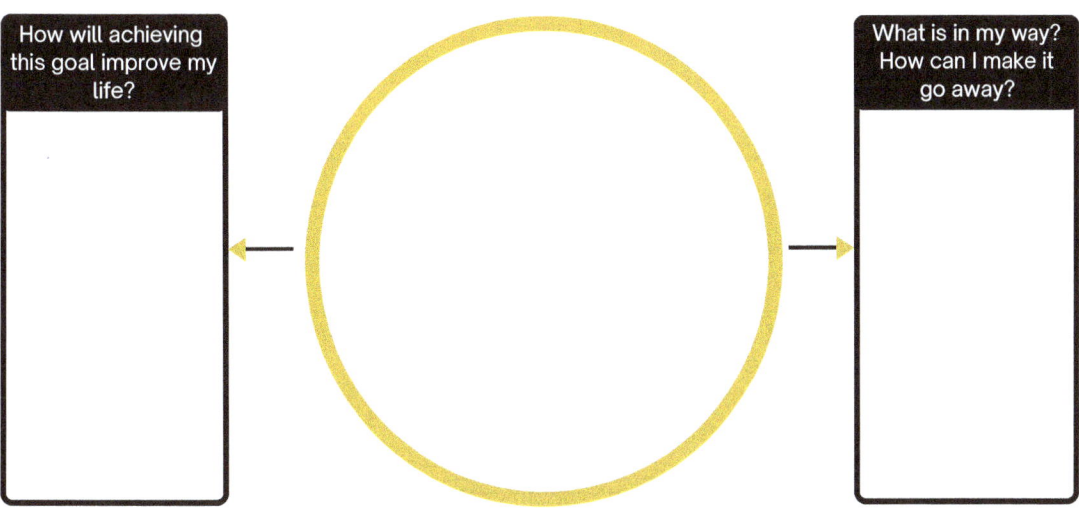

How will achieving this goal improve my life?

What is in my way? How can I make it go away?

ACTION STEPS

1
- _____
- _____
- _____
- _____

2
- _____
- _____
- _____
- _____

3
- _____
- _____
- _____
- _____

4
- _____
- _____
- _____
- _____

Time I am willing to set aside to complete my tasks: _____

Month:

SUNDAY	MONDAY	TUESDAY	WEDNESDAY	THURSDAY	FRIDAY	SATURDAY

GOALS

AFFIRMATION

PRIORITIES

NOTES

APPOINTMENTS	IMPORTANT DATES	BIRTHDAYS	SPECIAL EVENTS
_____	_____	_____	_____
_____	_____	_____	_____
_____	_____	_____	_____
_____	_____	_____	_____
_____	_____	_____	_____

THIS MONTH I WILL EXPAND MY KNOWLEDGE AND LEARN ABOUT

Monthly Book List

BOOK	BOOK	BOOK	BOOK
☆☆☆☆☆ ☐	☆☆☆☆☆ ☐	☆☆☆☆☆ ☐	☆☆☆☆☆ ☐
Progress	Progress	Progress	Progress

Identify the habits that you will practice daily to help you achieve your monthly goals.

HABIT TRACKER	1	2	3	4	5	6	7	8	9	10	11	12	13	14	15	16	17	18	19	20	21	22	23	24	25	26	27	28	29	30	31

Week:

MONDAY	TUESDAY	WEDNESDAY

THURSDAY	FRIDAY	SATURDAY

SUNDAY

PASSION. PURPOSE. PROGRESS. NEVER STOP GROWING!

This Week I am Grateful for:

TO DO:

APPOINTMENTS

MEALS

M
T
W
TH
F
S
SU

SHOPPING LIST

NOTES

Weekly Reflection

On a scale of 1-10, rate your week. - 1 2 3 4 5 6 7 8 9 10

How am I feeling? Why do I feel this way?

What went well this week? How am I progressing?

This week I learned:

I would like to improve on:

Things I am proud of?

Weekly Reflection

Things I need to let go of?

What habits did I maintain?

What habits were difficult for me to maintain?

How can I make next week better?

What will be realistic targets for next week? Do I need to revise my objectives

Week:

MONDAY	TUESDAY	WEDNESDAY

THURSDAY	FRIDAY	SATURDAY

SUNDAY

PASSION. PURPOSE. PROGRESS. NEVER STOP GROWING!

This Week I am Grateful for:

TO DO:

- _____
- _____
- _____
- _____
- _____
- _____
- _____

- _____
- _____
- _____
- _____
- _____
- _____
- _____

- _____
- _____
- _____
- _____
- _____
- _____
- _____

APPOINTMENTS

- _____
- _____
- _____
- _____
- _____
- _____
- _____
- _____

MEALS

M _____
T _____
W _____
TH _____
F _____
S _____
SU _____

SHOPPING LIST

- _____
- _____
- _____
- _____
- _____
- _____
- _____
- _____

NOTES

Weekly Reflection

On a scale of 1-10, rate your week. - 1 2 3 4 5 6 7 8 9 10

How am I feeling? Why do I feel this way?

What went well this week? How am I progressing?

This week I learned:

I would like to improve on:

Things I am proud of?

Weekly Reflection

Things I need to let go of?

What habits did I maintain?

What habits were difficult for me to maintain?

How can I make next week better?

What will be realistic targets for next week? Do I need to revise my objectives

Week:

MONDAY	TUESDAY	WEDNESDAY

THURSDAY	FRIDAY	SATURDAY

SUNDAY

PASSION. PURPOSE. PROGRESS. NEVER STOP GROWING!

This Week I am Grateful for:

TO DO:

- _____
- _____
- _____
- _____
- _____
- _____
- _____

- _____
- _____
- _____
- _____
- _____
- _____
- _____

- _____
- _____
- _____
- _____
- _____
- _____
- _____

APPOINTMENTS

- _____
- _____
- _____
- _____
- _____
- _____
- _____
- _____

MEALS

M _____
T _____
W _____
TH _____
F _____
S _____
SU _____

SHOPPING LIST

- _____
- _____
- _____
- _____
- _____
- _____
- _____
- _____

NOTES

Weekly Reflection

On a scale of 1-10, rate your week. - 1 2 3 4 5 6 7 8 9 10

How am I feeling? Why do I feel this way?

What went well this week? How am I progressing?

This week I learned:

I would like to improve on:

Things I am proud of?

Weekly Reflection

Things I need to let go of?

What habits did I maintain?

What habits were difficult for me to maintain?

How can I make next week better?

**What will be realistic targets for next week?
Do I need to revise my objectives**

Week:

MONDAY

TUESDAY

WEDNESDAY

THURSDAY

FRIDAY

SATURDAY

SUNDAY

PASSION. PURPOSE. PROGRESS. NEVER STOP GROWING!

This Week I am Grateful for:

TO DO:

-
-
-
-
-
-
-

-
-
-
-
-
-
-

-
-
-
-
-
-
-

APPOINTMENTS

-
-
-
-
-
-
-

MEALS

M
T
W
TH
F
S
SU

SHOPPING LIST

-
-
-
-
-
-
-

NOTES

Weekly Reflection

On a scale of 1-10, rate your week. - 1 2 3 4 5 6 7 8 9 10

How am I feeling? Why do I feel this way?

What went well this week? How am I progressing?

This week I learned:

I would like to improve on:

Things I am proud of?

Weekly Reflection

Things I need to let go of?

What habits did I maintain?

What habits were difficult for me to maintain?

How can I make next week better?

What will be realistic targets for next week? Do I need to revise my objectives

Week:

MONDAY	TUESDAY	WEDNESDAY

THURSDAY	FRIDAY	SATURDAY

SUNDAY

PASSION. PURPOSE. PROGRESS. NEVER STOP GROWING!

This Week I am Grateful for:

TO DO:

APPOINTMENTS

MEALS

M _____

T _____

W _____

TH _____

F _____

S _____

SU _____

SHOPPING LIST

NOTES

Weekly Reflection

On a scale of 1-10, rate your week. - 1 2 3 4 5 6 7 8 9 10

How am I feeling? Why do I feel this way?

What went well this week? How am I progressing?

This week I learned:

I would like to improve on:

Things I am proud of?

Weekly Reflection

Things I need to let go of?

What habits did I maintain?

What habits were difficult for me to maintain?

How can I make next week better?

What will be realistic targets for next week? Do I need to revise my objectives

I AM
Powerful

Monthly Reflection

What went well this month? How am I progressing?

Did I reach my goal? Why or why not?

How will I rate my efforts this month? How can I get better?

What will be realistic targets for next month? Do I need to revise my objectives?

Free space for notes sketching, mind-mapping and more.

SET A GOAL MAKE A PLAN. YOUR POSSIBILITIES ARE LIMITLESS.

Stay focused AT ALL TIMES.

30 Day CHALLENGE

This month I will challenge myself by:

1	2	3	4	5	6	7	8	9	10
11	12	13	14	15	16	17	18	19	20
21	22	23	24	25	26	27	28	29	30

My reason why:

Action Steps:

- _____
- _____
- _____

- _____
- _____

I will celebrate by:

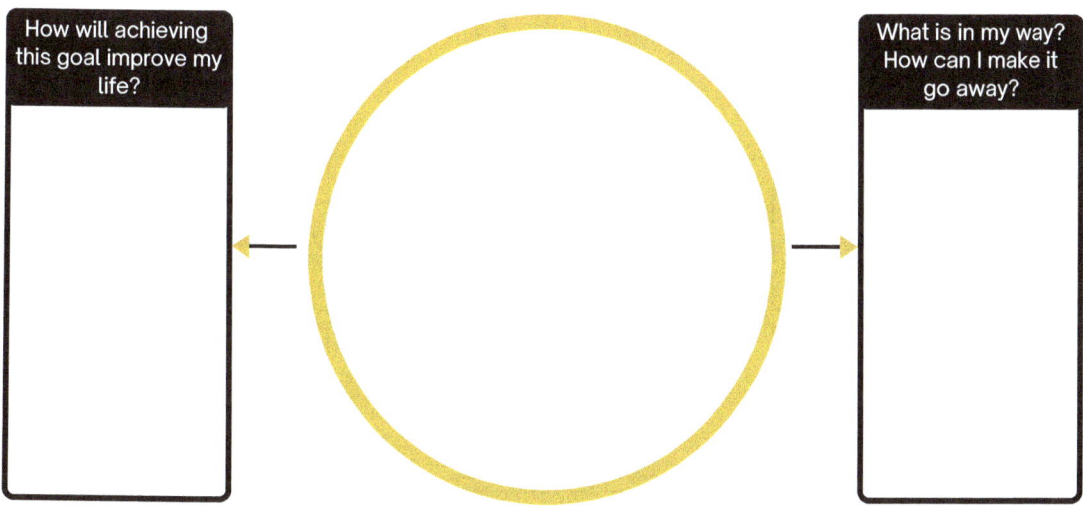

What is your number 1 goal for this month? Write it in the circle. Brainstorm 4 action steps that will help you towards your goal.

How will achieving this goal improve my life?

What is in my way? How can I make it go away?

ACTION STEPS

1
- _____
- _____
- _____
- _____

2
- _____
- _____
- _____
- _____

3
- _____
- _____
- _____
- _____

4
- _____
- _____
- _____
- _____

Time I am willing to set aside to complete my tasks: _____

Month:

SUNDAY	MONDAY	TUESDAY	WEDNESDAY	THURSDAY	FRIDAY	SATURDAY

GOALS

AFFIRMATION

PRIORITIES

NOTES

APPOINTMENTS	IMPORTANT DATES	BIRTHDAYS	SPECIAL EVENTS
_____	_____	_____	_____
_____	_____	_____	_____
_____	_____	_____	_____
_____	_____	_____	_____
_____	_____	_____	_____
_____	_____	_____	_____

THIS MONTH I WILL EXPAND MY KNOWLEDGE AND LEARN ABOUT

Monthly Book List

BOOK	BOOK	BOOK	BOOK
☆☆☆☆☆ ☐	☆☆☆☆☆ ☐	☆☆☆☆☆ ☐	☆☆☆☆☆ ☐
Progress	Progress	Progress	Progress

Identify the habits that you will practice daily to help you achieve your monthly goals.

HABIT TRACKER	1	2	3	4	5	6	7	8	9	10	11	12	13	14	15	16	17	18	19	20	21	22	23	24	25	26	27	28	29	30	31

Week:

MONDAY

TUESDAY

WEDNESDAY

THURSDAY

FRIDAY

SATURDAY

SUNDAY

PASSION. PURPOSE. PROGRESS. NEVER STOP GROWING!

This Week I am Grateful for:

TO DO:

APPOINTMENTS

MEALS

- M
- T
- W
- TH
- F
- S
- SU

SHOPPING LIST

NOTES

Weekly Reflection

On a scale of 1-10, rate your week. - 1 2 3 4 5 6 7 8 9 10

How am I feeling? Why do I feel this way?

What went well this week? How am I progressing?

This week I learned:

I would like to improve on:

Things I am proud of?

Weekly Reflection

Things I need to let go of?

What habits did I maintain?

What habits were difficult for me to maintain?

How can I make next week better?

What will be realistic targets for next week? Do I need to revise my objectives

Week:

MONDAY

TUESDAY

WEDNESDAY

THURSDAY

FRIDAY

SATURDAY

SUNDAY

PASSION. PURPOSE. PROGRESS. NEVER STOP GROWING!

This Week I am Grateful for:

TO DO:

APPOINTMENTS

MEALS

M
T
W
TH
F
S
SU

SHOPPING LIST

NOTES

Weekly Reflection

On a scale of 1-10, rate your week. - 1 2 3 4 5 6 7 8 9 10

How am I feeling? Why do I feel this way?

What went well this week? How am I progressing?

This week I learned:

I would like to improve on:

Things I am proud of?

Weekly Reflection

Things I need to let go of?

What habits did I maintain?

What habits were difficult for me to maintain?

How can I make next week better?

What will be realistic targets for next week? Do I need to revise my objectives

Week:

MONDAY

TUESDAY

WEDNESDAY

THURSDAY

FRIDAY

SATURDAY

SUNDAY

PASSION. PURPOSE. PROGRESS. NEVER STOP GROWING!

This Week I am Grateful for:

TO DO:

APPOINTMENTS

MEALS

M
T
W
TH
F
S
SU

SHOPPING LIST

NOTES

Weekly Reflection

On a scale of 1-10, rate your week. - 1 2 3 4 5 6 7 8 9 10

How am I feeling? Why do I feel this way?

What went well this week? How am I progressing?

This week I learned:

I would like to improve on:

Things I am proud of?

Weekly Reflection

Things I need to let go of?

What habits did I maintain?

What habits were difficult for me to maintain?

How can I make next week better?

What will be realistic targets for next week? Do I need to revise my objectives

Week:

MONDAY

TUESDAY

WEDNESDAY

THURSDAY

FRIDAY

SATURDAY

SUNDAY

PASSION. PURPOSE. PROGRESS. NEVER STOP GROWING!

This Week I am Grateful for:

TO DO:

APPOINTMENTS

MEALS

M
T
W
TH
F
S
SU

SHOPPING LIST

NOTES

Weekly Reflection

On a scale of 1-10, rate your week. - 1 2 3 4 5 6 7 8 9 10

How am I feeling? Why do I feel this way?

What went well this week? How am I progressing?

This week I learned:

I would like to improve on:

Things I am proud of?

Weekly Reflection

Things I need to let go of?

What habits did I maintain?

What habits were difficult for me to maintain?

How can I make next week better?

What will be realistic targets for next week? Do I need to revise my objectives

Week:

MONDAY

TUESDAY

WEDNESDAY

THURSDAY

FRIDAY

SATURDAY

SUNDAY

PASSION. PURPOSE. PROGRESS. NEVER STOP GROWING!

This Week I am Grateful for:

TO DO:

- _____
- _____
- _____
- _____
- _____
- _____
- _____

- _____
- _____
- _____
- _____
- _____
- _____
- _____

- _____
- _____
- _____
- _____
- _____
- _____
- _____

APPOINTMENTS

- _____
- _____
- _____
- _____
- _____
- _____
- _____
- _____

MEALS

M _____
T _____
W _____
TH _____
F _____
S _____
SU _____

SHOPPING LIST

- _____
- _____
- _____
- _____
- _____
- _____
- _____
- _____

NOTES

Weekly Reflection

On a scale of 1-10, rate your week. - 1 2 3 4 5 6 7 8 9 10

How am I feeling? Why do I feel this way?

What went well this week? How am I progressing?

This week I learned:

I would like to improve on:

Things I am proud of?

Weekly Reflection

Things I need to let go of?

What habits did I maintain?

What habits were difficult for me to maintain?

How can I make next week better?

What will be realistic targets for next week? Do I need to revise my objectives

I'M SUCCESSFUL IN EVERYTHING

I do

Monthly Reflection

What went well this month? How am I progressing?

Did I reach my goal? Why or why not?

How will I rate my efforts this month? How can I get better?

What will be realistic targets for next month? Do I need to revise my objectives?

Free space for notes sketching, mind-mapping and more.

SET A GOAL MAKE A PLAN. YOUR POSSIBILITIES ARE LIMITLESS.

You Can
YOU WILL!

30 Day CHALLENGE

This month I will challenge myself by:

1	2	3	4	5	6	7	8	9	10
11	12	13	14	15	16	17	18	19	20
21	22	23	24	25	26	27	28	29	30

My reason why:

Action Steps:

- _____
- _____
- _____

- _____
- _____

I will celebrate by:

What is your number 1 goal for this month? Write it in the circle. Brainstorm 4 action steps that will help you towards your goal.

How will achieving this goal improve my life?

What is in my way? How can I make it go away?

ACTION STEPS

1)
- _____
- _____
- _____
- _____

2)
- _____
- _____
- _____
- _____

3)
- _____
- _____
- _____
- _____

4)
- _____
- _____
- _____
- _____

Time I am willing to set aside to complete my tasks: _____

Month:

SUNDAY	MONDAY	TUESDAY	WEDNESDAY	THURSDAY	FRIDAY	SATURDAY

GOALS

AFFIRMATION

PRIORITIES

NOTES

APPOINTMENTS	IMPORTANT DATES	BIRTHDAYS	SPECIAL EVENTS
_____	_____	_____	_____
_____	_____	_____	_____
_____	_____	_____	_____
_____	_____	_____	_____
_____	_____	_____	_____

THIS MONTH I WILL EXPAND MY KNOWLEDGE AND LEARN ABOUT

Monthly Book List

BOOK	BOOK	BOOK	BOOK
☆☆☆☆☆ ☐	☆☆☆☆☆ ☐	☆☆☆☆☆ ☐	☆☆☆☆☆ ☐
Progress	Progress	Progress	Progress

Identify the habits that you will practice daily to help you achieve your monthly goals.

HABIT TRACKER	1	2	3	4	5	6	7	8	9	10	11	12	13	14	15	16	17	18	19	20	21	22	23	24	25	26	27	28	29	30	31

Week:

MONDAY	TUESDAY	WEDNESDAY

THURSDAY	FRIDAY	SATURDAY

SUNDAY

PASSION. PURPOSE. PROGRESS. NEVER STOP GROWING!

This Week I am Grateful for:

TO DO:

APPOINTMENTS

MEALS

M
T
W
TH
F
S
SU

SHOPPING LIST

NOTES

Weekly Reflection

On a scale of 1-10, rate your week. - 1 2 3 4 5 6 7 8 9 10

How am I feeling? Why do I feel this way?

What went well this week? How am I progressing?

This week I learned:

I would like to improve on:

Things I am proud of?

Weekly Reflection

Things I need to let go of?

What habits did I maintain?

What habits were difficult for me to maintain?

How can I make next week better?

What will be realistic targets for next week? Do I need to revise my objectives

Week:

MONDAY	TUESDAY	WEDNESDAY

THURSDAY	FRIDAY	SATURDAY

SUNDAY

PASSION. PURPOSE. PROGRESS. NEVER STOP GROWING!

This Week I am Grateful for:

TO DO:

APPOINTMENTS

MEALS

M
T
W
TH
F
S
SU

SHOPPING LIST

NOTES

Weekly Reflection

On a scale of 1-10, rate your week. - 1 2 3 4 5 6 7 8 9 10

How am I feeling? Why do I feel this way?

What went well this week? How am I progressing?

This week I learned:

I would like to improve on:

Things I am proud of?

Weekly Reflection

Things I need to let go of?

What habits did I maintain?

What habits were difficult for me to maintain?

How can I make next week better?

What will be realistic targets for next week? Do I need to revise my objectives

Week:

MONDAY

TUESDAY

WEDNESDAY

THURSDAY

FRIDAY

SATURDAY

SUNDAY

PASSION. PURPOSE. PROGRESS. NEVER STOP GROWING!

This Week I am Grateful for:

TO DO:

- _____
- _____
- _____
- _____
- _____
- _____
- _____

- _____
- _____
- _____
- _____
- _____
- _____

- _____
- _____
- _____
- _____
- _____
- _____
- _____

APPOINTMENTS

- _____
- _____
- _____
- _____
- _____
- _____
- _____
- _____

MEALS

M _____
T _____
W _____
TH _____
F _____
S _____
SU _____

SHOPPING LIST

- _____
- _____
- _____
- _____
- _____
- _____
- _____

NOTES

Weekly Reflection

On a scale of 1-10, rate your week. - 1 2 3 4 5 6 7 8 9 10

How am I feeling? Why do I feel this way?

What went well this week? How am I progressing?

This week I learned:

I would like to improve on:

Things I am proud of?

Weekly Reflection

Things I need to let go of?

What habits did I maintain?

What habits were difficult for me to maintain?

How can I make next week better?

What will be realistic targets for next week? Do I need to revise my objectives

Week:

MONDAY	TUESDAY	WEDNESDAY

THURSDAY	FRIDAY	SATURDAY

SUNDAY

PASSION. PURPOSE. PROGRESS. NEVER STOP GROWING!

This Week I am Grateful for:

TO DO:

APPOINTMENTS	MEALS	SHOPPING LIST
	M	
	T	
	W	
	TH	
	F	
	S	
	SU	

NOTES

Weekly Reflection

On a scale of 1-10, rate your week. - 1 2 3 4 5 6 7 8 9 10

How am I feeling? Why do I feel this way?

What went well this week? How am I progressing?

This week I learned:

I would like to improve on:

Things I am proud of?

Weekly Reflection

Things I need to let go of?

What habits did I maintain?

What habits were difficult for me to maintain?

How can I make next week better?

What will be realistic targets for next week? Do I need to revise my objectives

Week:

MONDAY	TUESDAY	WEDNESDAY

THURSDAY	FRIDAY	SATURDAY

SUNDAY

PASSION. PURPOSE. PROGRESS. NEVER STOP GROWING!

This Week I am Grateful for:

TO DO:

APPOINTMENTS

MEALS

- M
- T
- W
- TH
- F
- S
- SU

SHOPPING LIST

NOTES

Weekly Reflection

On a scale of 1-10, rate your week. - 1 2 3 4 5 6 7 8 9 10

How am I feeling? Why do I feel this way?

What went well this week? How am I progressing?

This week I learned:

I would like to improve on:

Things I am proud of?

Weekly Reflection

Things I need to let go of?

What habits did I maintain?

What habits were difficult for me to maintain?

How can I make next week better?

What will be realistic targets for next week? Do I need to revise my objectives

THERE ARE *No Limits* TO WHAT I CAN DO

Monthly Reflection

What went well this month? How am I progressing?

Did I reach my goal? Why or why not?

How will I rate my efforts this month? How can I get better?

What will be realistic targets for next month? Do I need to revise my objectives?

Free space for notes sketching, mind-mapping and more.

SET A GOAL MAKE A PLAN. YOUR POSSIBILITIES ARE LIMITLESS.

Be
UNSTOPPABLE

30 Day CHALLENGE

This month I will challenge myself by:

1	2	3	4	5	6	7	8	9	10
11	12	13	14	15	16	17	18	19	20
21	22	23	24	25	26	27	28	29	30

My reason why:

Action Steps:

- _____
- _____
- _____

- _____
- _____
- _____

I will celebrate by:

What is your number 1 goal for this month? Write it in the circle. Brainstorm 4 action steps that will help you towards your goal.

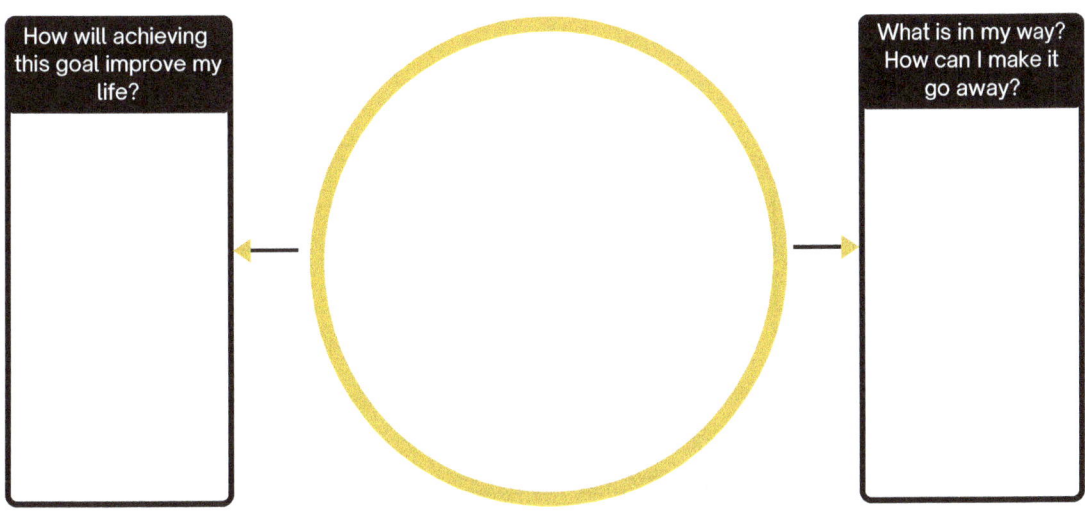

How will achieving this goal improve my life?

What is in my way? How can I make it go away?

ACTION STEPS

1
- _____
- _____
- _____
- _____

2
- _____
- _____
- _____
- _____

3
- _____
- _____
- _____
- _____

4
- _____
- _____
- _____
- _____

Time I am willing to set aside to complete my tasks: _____

Month:

SUNDAY	MONDAY	TUESDAY	WEDNESDAY	THURSDAY	FRIDAY	SATURDAY

GOALS

AFFIRMATION

PRIORITIES

NOTES

APPOINTMENTS	IMPORTANT DATES	BIRTHDAYS	SPECIAL EVENTS
_____	_____	_____	_____
_____	_____	_____	_____
_____	_____	_____	_____
_____	_____	_____	_____
_____	_____	_____	_____

THIS MONTH I WILL EXPAND MY KNOWLEDGE AND LEARN ABOUT

Monthly Book List

BOOK	BOOK	BOOK	BOOK
☆☆☆☆☆ ☐	☆☆☆☆☆ ☐	☆☆☆☆☆ ☐	☆☆☆☆☆ ☐
Progress	Progress	Progress	Progress

Identify the habits that you will practice daily to help you achieve your monthly goals.

HABIT TRACKER	1	2	3	4	5	6	7	8	9	10	11	12	13	14	15	16	17	18	19	20	21	22	23	24	25	26	27	28	29	30	31

Week:

MONDAY

TUESDAY

WEDNESDAY

THURSDAY

FRIDAY

SATURDAY

SUNDAY

PASSION. PURPOSE. PROGRESS. NEVER STOP GROWING!

This Week I am Grateful for:

TO DO:

- _____
- _____
- _____
- _____
- _____
- _____
- _____

- _____
- _____
- _____
- _____
- _____
- _____
- _____

- _____
- _____
- _____
- _____
- _____
- _____
- _____

APPOINTMENTS

- _____
- _____
- _____
- _____
- _____
- _____
- _____

MEALS

M _____
T _____
W _____
TH _____
F _____
S _____
SU _____

SHOPPING LIST

- _____
- _____
- _____
- _____
- _____
- _____
- _____

NOTES

Weekly Reflection

On a scale of 1-10, rate your week. - 1 2 3 4 5 6 7 8 9 10

How am I feeling? Why do I feel this way?

What went well this week? How am I progressing?

This week I learned:

I would like to improve on:

Things I am proud of?

Weekly Reflection

Things I need to let go of?

What habits did I maintain?

What habits were difficult for me to maintain?

How can I make next week better?

What will be realistic targets for next week? Do I need to revise my objectives

Week:

MONDAY

TUESDAY

WEDNESDAY

THURSDAY

FRIDAY

SATURDAY

SUNDAY

PASSION. PURPOSE. PROGRESS. NEVER STOP GROWING!

This Week I am Grateful for:

TO DO:

APPOINTMENTS

MEALS

M
T
W
TH
F
S
SU

SHOPPING LIST

NOTES

Weekly Reflection

On a scale of 1-10, rate your week. - 1 2 3 4 5 6 7 8 9 10

How am I feeling? Why do I feel this way?

What went well this week? How am I progressing?

This week I learned:

I would like to improve on:

Things I am proud of?

Weekly Reflection

Things I need to let go of?

What habits did I maintain?

What habits were difficult for me to maintain?

How can I make next week better?

What will be realistic targets for next week? Do I need to revise my objectives

Week:

MONDAY

TUESDAY

WEDNESDAY

THURSDAY

FRIDAY

SATURDAY

SUNDAY

PASSION. PURPOSE. PROGRESS. NEVER STOP GROWING!

This Week I am Grateful for:

TO DO:

APPOINTMENTS

MEALS

M
T
W
TH
F
S
SU

SHOPPING LIST

NOTES

Weekly Reflection

On a scale of 1-10, rate your week. - 1 2 3 4 5 6 7 8 9 10

How am I feeling? Why do I feel this way?

What went well this week? How am I progressing?

This week I learned:

I would like to improve on:

Things I am proud of?

Weekly Reflection

Things I need to let go of?

What habits did I maintain?

What habits were difficult for me to maintain?

How can I make next week better?

What will be realistic targets for next week? Do I need to revise my objectives

Week:

MONDAY	TUESDAY	WEDNESDAY

THURSDAY	FRIDAY	SATURDAY

SUNDAY

PASSION. PURPOSE. PROGRESS. NEVER STOP GROWING!

This Week I am Grateful for:

TO DO:

APPOINTMENTS

MEALS

M
T
W
TH
F
S
SU

SHOPPING LIST

NOTES

Weekly Reflection

On a scale of 1-10, rate your week. - 1 2 3 4 5 6 7 8 9 10

How am I feeling? Why do I feel this way?

What went well this week? How am I progressing?

This week I learned:

I would like to improve on:

Things I am proud of?

Weekly Reflection

Things I need to let go of?

What habits did I maintain?

What habits were difficult for me to maintain?

How can I make next week better?

**What will be realistic targets for next week?
Do I need to revise my objectives**

Week:

MONDAY

TUESDAY

WEDNESDAY

THURSDAY

FRIDAY

SATURDAY

SUNDAY

PASSION. PURPOSE. PROGRESS. NEVER STOP GROWING!

This Week I am Grateful for:

TO DO:

- _____
- _____
- _____
- _____
- _____
- _____
- _____

- _____
- _____
- _____
- _____
- _____
- _____
- _____

- _____
- _____
- _____
- _____
- _____
- _____
- _____

APPOINTMENTS

- _____
- _____
- _____
- _____
- _____
- _____
- _____
- _____
- _____

MEALS

M _____
T _____
W _____
TH _____
F _____
S _____
SU _____

SHOPPING LIST

- _____
- _____
- _____
- _____
- _____
- _____
- _____
- _____
- _____

NOTES

Weekly Reflection

On a scale of 1-10, rate your week. - 1 2 3 4 5 6 7 8 9 10

How am I feeling? Why do I feel this way?

What went well this week? How am I progressing?

This week I learned:

I would like to improve on:

Things I am proud of?

Weekly Reflection

Things I need to let go of?

What habits did I maintain?

What habits were difficult for me to maintain?

How can I make next week better?

What will be realistic targets for next week? Do I need to revise my objectives

I AM
learning
& GROWING

Monthly Reflection

What went well this month? How am I progressing?

Did I reach my goal? Why or why not?

How will I rate my efforts this month? How can I get better?

What will be realistic targets for next month? Do I need to revise my objectives?

Free space for notes sketching, mind-mapping and more.

SET A GOAL MAKE A PLAN. YOUR POSSIBILITIES ARE LIMITLESS.

Trust Yourself

trust the timing of your life...

30 Day CHALLENGE

This month I will challenge myself by:

1	2	3	4	5	6	7	8	9	10
11	12	13	14	15	16	17	18	19	20
21	22	23	24	25	26	27	28	29	30

My reason why:

Action Steps:

- _____
- _____
- _____

- _____
- _____
- _____

I will celebrate by:

What is your number 1 goal for this month? Write it in the circle. Brainstorm 4 action steps that will help you towards your goal.

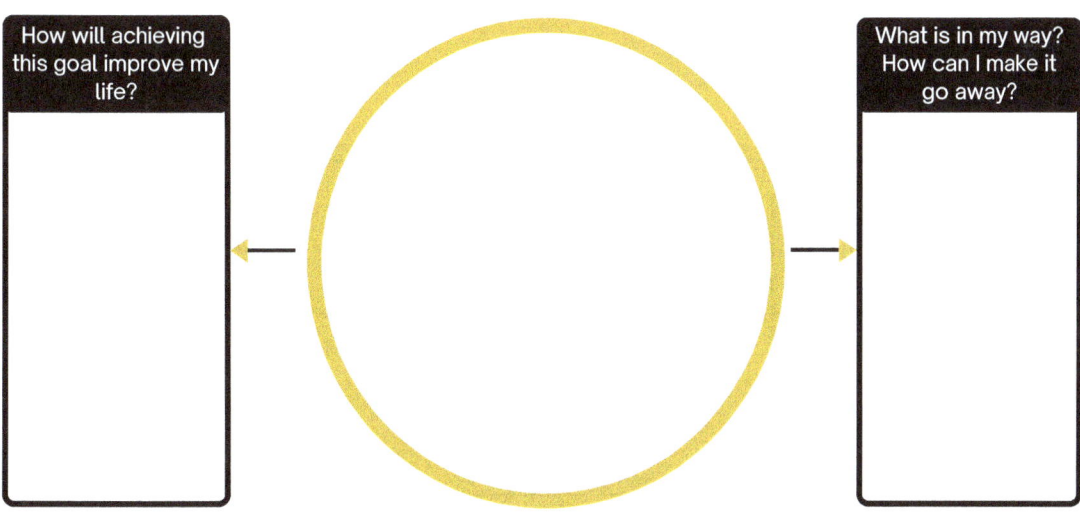

How will achieving this goal improve my life?		What is in my way? How can I make it go away?

ACTION STEPS

1
- _____
- _____
- _____
- _____

2
- _____
- _____
- _____
- _____

3
- _____
- _____
- _____
- _____

4
- _____
- _____
- _____
- _____

Time I am willing to set aside to complete my tasks: _____

Month:

SUNDAY	MONDAY	TUESDAY	WEDNESDAY	THURSDAY	FRIDAY	SATURDAY

GOALS

AFFIRMATION

PRIORITIES

NOTES

APPOINTMENTS	IMPORTANT DATES	BIRTHDAYS	SPECIAL EVENTS
_____	_____	_____	_____
_____	_____	_____	_____
_____	_____	_____	_____
_____	_____	_____	_____
_____	_____	_____	_____

THIS MONTH I WILL EXPAND MY KNOWLEDGE AND LEARN ABOUT

Monthly Book List

BOOK	BOOK	BOOK	BOOK
☆☆☆☆☆	☆☆☆☆☆	☆☆☆☆☆	☆☆☆☆☆
Progress	Progress	Progress	Progress

Identify the habits that you will practice daily to help you achieve your monthly goals.

HABIT TRACKER	1	2	3	4	5	6	7	8	9	10	11	12	13	14	15	16	17	18	19	20	21	22	23	24	25	26	27	28	29	30	31

Week:

MONDAY

TUESDAY

WEDNESDAY

THURSDAY

FRIDAY

SATURDAY

SUNDAY

PASSION. PURPOSE. PROGRESS. NEVER STOP GROWING!

This Week I am Grateful for:

TO DO:

- _____
- _____
- _____
- _____
- _____
- _____
- _____

- _____
- _____
- _____
- _____
- _____
- _____
- _____

- _____
- _____
- _____
- _____
- _____
- _____
- _____

APPOINTMENTS

- _____
- _____
- _____
- _____
- _____
- _____
- _____
- _____

MEALS

M _____
T _____
W _____
TH _____
F _____
S _____
SU _____

SHOPPING LIST

- _____
- _____
- _____
- _____
- _____
- _____
- _____
- _____

NOTES

Weekly Reflection

On a scale of 1-10, rate your week. - 1 2 3 4 5 6 7 8 9 10

How am I feeling? Why do I feel this way?

What went well this week? How am I progressing?

This week I learned:

I would like to improve on:

Things I am proud of?

Weekly Reflection

Things I need to let go of?

What habits did I maintain?

What habits were difficult for me to maintain?

How can I make next week better?

What will be realistic targets for next week?
Do I need to revise my objectives

Week:

MONDAY

TUESDAY

WEDNESDAY

THURSDAY

FRIDAY

SATURDAY

SUNDAY

PASSION. PURPOSE. PROGRESS. NEVER STOP GROWING!

This Week I am Grateful for:

TO DO:

- _____
- _____
- _____
- _____
- _____
- _____
- _____

- _____
- _____
- _____
- _____
- _____
- _____
- _____

- _____
- _____
- _____
- _____
- _____
- _____
- _____

APPOINTMENTS

- _____
- _____
- _____
- _____
- _____
- _____
- _____
- _____

MEALS

M _____
T _____
W _____
TH _____
F _____
S _____
SU _____

SHOPPING LIST

- _____
- _____
- _____
- _____
- _____
- _____
- _____
- _____

NOTES

Weekly Reflection

On a scale of 1-10, rate your week. - 1 2 3 4 5 6 7 8 9 10

How am I feeling? Why do I feel this way?

What went well this week? How am I progressing?

This week I learned:

I would like to improve on:

Things I am proud of?

Weekly Reflection

Things I need to let go of?

What habits did I maintain?

What habits were difficult for me to maintain?

How can I make next week better?

**What will be realistic targets for next week?
Do I need to revise my objectives**

Week:

MONDAY	TUESDAY	WEDNESDAY

THURSDAY	FRIDAY	SATURDAY

SUNDAY

PASSION. PURPOSE. PROGRESS. NEVER STOP GROWING!

This Week I am Grateful for:

TO DO:

- _____
- _____
- _____
- _____
- _____
- _____
- _____

- _____
- _____
- _____
- _____
- _____
- _____
- _____

- _____
- _____
- _____
- _____
- _____
- _____
- _____

APPOINTMENTS

- _____
- _____
- _____
- _____
- _____
- _____
- _____
- _____

MEALS

M _____
T _____
W _____
TH _____
F _____
S _____
SU _____

SHOPPING LIST

- _____
- _____
- _____
- _____
- _____
- _____
- _____
- _____

NOTES

Weekly Reflection

On a scale of 1-10, rate your week. - 1 2 3 4 5 6 7 8 9 10

How am I feeling? Why do I feel this way?

What went well this week? How am I progressing?

This week I learned:

I would like to improve on:

Things I am proud of?

Weekly Reflection

Things I need to let go of?

What habits did I maintain?

What habits were difficult for me to maintain?

How can I make next week better?

**What will be realistic targets for next week?
Do I need to revise my objectives**

Week:

MONDAY	TUESDAY	WEDNESDAY

THURSDAY	FRIDAY	SATURDAY

SUNDAY

PASSION. PURPOSE. PROGRESS. NEVER STOP GROWING!

This Week I am Grateful for:

TO DO:

APPOINTMENTS

MEALS

- M
- T
- W
- TH
- F
- S
- SU

SHOPPING LIST

NOTES

Weekly Reflection

On a scale of 1-10, rate your week. - 1 2 3 4 5 6 7 8 9 10

How am I feeling? Why do I feel this way?

What went well this week? How am I progressing?

This week I learned:

I would like to improve on:

Things I am proud of?

Weekly Reflection

Things I need to let go of?

What habits did I maintain?

What habits were difficult for me to maintain?

How can I make next week better?

What will be realistic targets for next week? Do I need to revise my objectives

Week:

MONDAY

TUESDAY

WEDNESDAY

THURSDAY

FRIDAY

SATURDAY

SUNDAY

PASSION. PURPOSE. PROGRESS. NEVER STOP GROWING!

This Week I am Grateful for:

TO DO:

- _____
- _____
- _____
- _____
- _____
- _____
- _____

- _____
- _____
- _____
- _____
- _____
- _____
- _____

APPOINTMENTS

- _____
- _____
- _____
- _____
- _____
- _____
- _____
- _____

MEALS

M _____
T _____
W _____
TH _____
F _____
S _____
SU _____

SHOPPING LIST

- _____
- _____
- _____
- _____
- _____
- _____
- _____
- _____

NOTES

Weekly Reflection

On a scale of 1-10, rate your week. - 1 2 3 4 5 6 7 8 9 10

How am I feeling? Why do I feel this way?

What went well this week? How am I progressing?

This week I learned:

I would like to improve on:

Things I am proud of?

Weekly Reflection

Things I need to let go of?

What habits did I maintain?

What habits were difficult for me to maintain?

How can I make next week better?

What will be realistic targets for next week? Do I need to revise my objectives

NO MATTER HOW MANY TIMES THE WORLD TRIES TO KNOCK ME DOWN I'LL ALWAYS

Monthly Reflection

What went well this month? How am I progressing?

Did I reach my goal? Why or why not?

How will I rate my efforts this month? How can I get better?

What will be realistic targets for next month? Do I need to revise my objectives?

Free space for notes sketching, mind-mapping and more.

SET A GOAL MAKE A PLAN. YOUR POSSIBILITIES ARE LIMITLESS.

I HAVE *the Power* TO CREATE *the life* I DESERVE

30 Day CHALLENGE

This month I will challenge myself by:

1	2	3	4	5	6	7	8	9	10
11	12	13	14	15	16	17	18	19	20
21	22	23	24	25	26	27	28	29	30

My reason why:

Action Steps:

- _____
- _____
- _____

- _____
- _____
- _____

I will celebrate by:

What is your number 1 goal for this month? Write it in the circle. Brainstorm 4 action steps that will help you towards your goal.

How will achieving this goal improve my life?

What is in my way? How can I make it go away?

ACTION STEPS

1
- _____
- _____
- _____
- _____

2
- _____
- _____
- _____
- _____

3
- _____
- _____
- _____
- _____

4
- _____
- _____
- _____
- _____

Time I am willing to set aside to complete my tasks: _____

Month:

SUNDAY	MONDAY	TUESDAY	WEDNESDAY	THURSDAY	FRIDAY	SATURDAY

GOALS

AFFIRMATION

PRIORITIES

NOTES

APPOINTMENTS	IMPORTANT DATES	BIRTHDAYS	SPECIAL EVENTS
_____	_____	_____	_____
_____	_____	_____	_____
_____	_____	_____	_____
_____	_____	_____	_____
_____	_____	_____	_____

THIS MONTH I WILL EXPAND MY KNOWLEDGE AND LEARN ABOUT

Monthly Book List

BOOK	BOOK	BOOK	BOOK
☆☆☆☆☆ ☐	☆☆☆☆☆ ☐	☆☆☆☆☆ ☐	☆☆☆☆☆ ☐
Progress	Progress	Progress	Progress

Identify the habits that you will practice daily to help you achieve your monthly goals.

HABIT TRACKER	1	2	3	4	5	6	7	8	9	10	11	12	13	14	15	16	17	18	19	20	21	22	23	24	25	26	27	28	29	30	31

Week:

MONDAY

TUESDAY

WEDNESDAY

THURSDAY

FRIDAY

SATURDAY

SUNDAY

PASSION. PURPOSE. PROGRESS. NEVER STOP GROWING!

This Week I am Grateful for:

TO DO:

- _____
- _____
- _____
- _____
- _____
- _____
- _____

- _____
- _____
- _____
- _____
- _____
- _____
- _____

- _____
- _____
- _____
- _____
- _____
- _____
- _____

APPOINTMENTS

- _____
- _____
- _____
- _____
- _____
- _____
- _____
- _____

MEALS

M _____
T _____
W _____
TH _____
F _____
S _____
SU _____

SHOPPING LIST

- _____
- _____
- _____
- _____
- _____
- _____
- _____
- _____

NOTES

Weekly Reflection

On a scale of 1-10, rate your week. - 1 2 3 4 5 6 7 8 9 10

How am I feeling? Why do I feel this way?

What went well this week? How am I progressing?

This week I learned:

I would like to improve on:

Things I am proud of?

Weekly Reflection

Things I need to let go of?

What habits did I maintain?

What habits were difficult for me to maintain?

How can I make next week better?

What will be realistic targets for next week? Do I need to revise my objectives

Week:

MONDAY

TUESDAY

WEDNESDAY

THURSDAY

FRIDAY

SATURDAY

SUNDAY

PASSION. PURPOSE. PROGRESS. NEVER STOP GROWING!

This Week I am Grateful for:

TO DO:

APPOINTMENTS

MEALS

M
T
W
TH
F
S
SU

SHOPPING LIST

NOTES

Weekly Reflection

On a scale of 1-10, rate your week. - 1 2 3 4 5 6 7 8 9 10

How am I feeling? Why do I feel this way?

What went well this week? How am I progressing?

This week I learned:

I would like to improve on:

Things I am proud of?

Weekly Reflection

Things I need to let go of?

What habits did I maintain?

What habits were difficult for me to maintain?

How can I make next week better?

**What will be realistic targets for next week?
Do I need to revise my objectives**

Week:

MONDAY

TUESDAY

WEDNESDAY

THURSDAY

FRIDAY

SATURDAY

SUNDAY

PASSION. PURPOSE. PROGRESS. NEVER STOP GROWING!

This Week I am Grateful for:

TO DO:

APPOINTMENTS

MEALS

M
T
W
TH
F
S
SU

SHOPPING LIST

NOTES

Weekly Reflection

On a scale of 1-10, rate your week. - 1 2 3 4 5 6 7 8 9 10

How am I feeling? Why do I feel this way?

What went well this week? How am I progressing?

This week I learned:

I would like to improve on:

Things I am proud of?

Weekly Reflection

Things I need to let go of?

What habits did I maintain?

What habits were difficult for me to maintain?

How can I make next week better?

What will be realistic targets for next week? Do I need to revise my objectives

Week:

MONDAY

TUESDAY

WEDNESDAY

THURSDAY

FRIDAY

SATURDAY

SUNDAY

PASSION. PURPOSE. PROGRESS. NEVER STOP GROWING!

This Week I am Grateful for:

TO DO:

APPOINTMENTS

MEALS

- M
- T
- W
- TH
- F
- S
- SU

SHOPPING LIST

NOTES

Weekly Reflection

On a scale of 1-10, rate your week. - 1 2 3 4 5 6 7 8 9 10

How am I feeling? Why do I feel this way?

What went well this week? How am I progressing?

This week I learned:

I would like to improve on:

Things I am proud of?

Weekly Reflection

Things I need to let go of?

What habits did I maintain?

What habits were difficult for me to maintain?

How can I make next week better?

**What will be realistic targets for next week?
Do I need to revise my objectives**

Week:

MONDAY

TUESDAY

WEDNESDAY

THURSDAY

FRIDAY

SATURDAY

SUNDAY

PASSION. PURPOSE. PROGRESS. NEVER STOP GROWING!

This Week I am Grateful for:

TO DO:

- _____
- _____
- _____
- _____
- _____
- _____
- _____

- _____
- _____
- _____
- _____
- _____
- _____
- _____

- _____
- _____
- _____
- _____
- _____
- _____
- _____

APPOINTMENTS

- _____
- _____
- _____
- _____
- _____
- _____
- _____
- _____

MEALS

M _____

T _____

W _____

TH _____

F _____

S _____

SU _____

SHOPPING LIST

- _____
- _____
- _____
- _____
- _____
- _____
- _____
- _____

NOTES

Weekly Reflection

On a scale of 1-10, rate your week. - 1 2 3 4 5 6 7 8 9 10

How am I feeling? Why do I feel this way?

What went well this week? How am I progressing?

This week I learned:

I would like to improve on:

Things I am proud of?

Weekly Reflection

Things I need to let go of?

What habits did I maintain?

What habits were difficult for me to maintain?

How can I make next week better?

**What will be realistic targets for next week?
Do I need to revise my objectives**

YOU GET WHAT YOU FOCUS ON SO FOCUS ON WHAT YOU WANT

Monthly Reflection

What went well this month? How am I progressing?

Did I reach my goal? Why or why not?

How will I rate my efforts this month? How can I get better?

What will be realistic targets for next month? Do I need to revise my objectives?

Free space for notes sketching, mind-mapping and more.

SET A GOAL MAKE A PLAN. YOUR POSSIBILITIES ARE LIMITLESS.

I DREAM
I Believe
I RECEIVE

30 Day CHALLENGE

This month I will challenge myself by:

1	2	3	4	5	6	7	8	9	10
11	12	13	14	15	16	17	18	19	20
21	22	23	24	25	26	27	28	29	30

My reason why:

Action Steps:

- _____
- _____
- _____

- _____
- _____
- _____

I will celebrate by:

What is your number 1 goal for this month? Write it in the circle. Brainstorm 4 action steps that will help you towards your goal.

How will achieving this goal improve my life?

What is in my way? How can I make it go away?

ACTION STEPS

1
- _____
- _____
- _____
- _____

2
- _____
- _____
- _____
- _____

3
- _____
- _____
- _____
- _____

4
- _____
- _____
- _____
- _____

Time I am willing to set aside to complete my tasks: _____

Month:

SUNDAY	MONDAY	TUESDAY	WEDNESDAY	THURSDAY	FRIDAY	SATURDAY

GOALS

AFFIRMATION

PRIORITIES

NOTES

APPOINTMENTS	IMPORTANT DATES	BIRTHDAYS	SPECIAL EVENTS
_____	_____	_____	_____
_____	_____	_____	_____
_____	_____	_____	_____
_____	_____	_____	_____
_____	_____	_____	_____

THIS MONTH I WILL EXPAND MY KNOWLEDGE AND LEARN ABOUT

Monthly Book List

BOOK	BOOK	BOOK	BOOK
☆☆☆☆☆ ☐	☆☆☆☆☆ ☐	☆☆☆☆☆ ☐	☆☆☆☆☆ ☐
Progress	Progress	Progress	Progress

Identify the habits that you will practice daily to help you achieve your monthly goals.

HABIT TRACKER	1	2	3	4	5	6	7	8	9	10	11	12	13	14	15	16	17	18	19	20	21	22	23	24	25	26	27	28	29	30	31

Week:

MONDAY	TUESDAY	WEDNESDAY

THURSDAY	FRIDAY	SATURDAY

SUNDAY

PASSION. PURPOSE. PROGRESS. NEVER STOP GROWING!

This Week I am Grateful for:

TO DO:

APPOINTMENTS

MEALS

- M
- T
- W
- TH
- F
- S
- SU

SHOPPING LIST

NOTES

Weekly Reflection

On a scale of 1-10, rate your week. - 1 2 3 4 5 6 7 8 9 10

How am I feeling? Why do I feel this way?

What went well this week? How am I progressing?

This week I learned:

I would like to improve on:

Things I am proud of?

Weekly Reflection

Things I need to let go of?

What habits did I maintain?

What habits were difficult for me to maintain?

How can I make next week better?

What will be realistic targets for next week? Do I need to revise my objectives

Week:

MONDAY	TUESDAY	WEDNESDAY

THURSDAY	FRIDAY	SATURDAY

SUNDAY

PASSION. PURPOSE. PROGRESS. NEVER STOP GROWING!

This Week I am Grateful for:

TO DO:

APPOINTMENTS

MEALS

M
T
W
TH
F
S
SU

SHOPPING LIST

NOTES

Weekly Reflection

On a scale of 1-10, rate your week. - 1 2 3 4 5 6 7 8 9 10

How am I feeling? Why do I feel this way?

What went well this week? How am I progressing?

This week I learned:

I would like to improve on:

Things I am proud of?

Weekly Reflection

Things I need to let go of?

What habits did I maintain?

What habits were difficult for me to maintain?

How can I make next week better?

What will be realistic targets for next week? Do I need to revise my objectives

Week:

MONDAY

TUESDAY

WEDNESDAY

THURSDAY

FRIDAY

SATURDAY

SUNDAY

PASSION. PURPOSE. PROGRESS. NEVER STOP GROWING!

This Week I am Grateful for:

TO DO:

APPOINTMENTS

MEALS

M
T
W
TH
F
S
SU

SHOPPING LIST

NOTES

Weekly Reflection

On a scale of 1-10, rate your week. - 1 2 3 4 5 6 7 8 9 10

How am I feeling? Why do I feel this way?

What went well this week? How am I progressing?

This week I learned:

I would like to improve on:

Things I am proud of?

Weekly Reflection

Things I need to let go of?

What habits did I maintain?

What habits were difficult for me to maintain?

How can I make next week better?

What will be realistic targets for next week? Do I need to revise my objectives

Week:

MONDAY

TUESDAY

WEDNESDAY

THURSDAY

FRIDAY

SATURDAY

SUNDAY

PASSION. PURPOSE. PROGRESS. NEVER STOP GROWING!

This Week I am Grateful for:

TO DO:

- _____
- _____
- _____
- _____
- _____
- _____

- _____
- _____
- _____
- _____
- _____
- _____

- _____
- _____
- _____
- _____
- _____
- _____

APPOINTMENTS

- _____
- _____
- _____
- _____
- _____
- _____
- _____
- _____

MEALS

M _____
T _____
W _____
TH _____
F _____
S _____
SU _____

SHOPPING LIST

- _____
- _____
- _____
- _____
- _____
- _____
- _____
- _____

NOTES

Weekly Reflection

On a scale of 1-10, rate your week. - 1 2 3 4 5 6 7 8 9 10

How am I feeling? Why do I feel this way?

What went well this week? How am I progressing?

This week I learned:

I would like to improve on:

Things I am proud of?

Weekly Reflection

Things I need to let go of?

What habits did I maintain?

What habits were difficult for me to maintain?

How can I make next week better?

**What will be realistic targets for next week?
Do I need to revise my objectives**

Week:

MONDAY

TUESDAY

WEDNESDAY

THURSDAY

FRIDAY

SATURDAY

SUNDAY

PASSION. PURPOSE. PROGRESS. NEVER STOP GROWING!

This Week I am Grateful for:

TO DO:

APPOINTMENTS

MEALS

M
T
W
TH
F
S
SU

SHOPPING LIST

NOTES

Weekly Reflection

On a scale of 1-10, rate your week. - 1 2 3 4 5 6 7 8 9 10

How am I feeling? Why do I feel this way?

What went well this week? How am I progressing?

This week I learned:

I would like to improve on:

Things I am proud of?

Weekly Reflection

Things I need to let go of?

What habits did I maintain?

What habits were difficult for me to maintain?

How can I make next week better?

**What will be realistic targets for next week?
Do I need to revise my objectives**

EVERYTHING I TOUCH TURNS INTO *Gold*

Monthly Reflection

What went well this month? How am I progressing?

Did I reach my goal? Why or why not?

How will I rate my efforts this month? How can I get better?

What will be realistic targets for next month? Do I need to revise my objectives?

Free space for notes sketching, mind-mapping and more.

SET A GOAL MAKE A PLAN. YOUR POSSIBILITIES ARE LIMITLESS.

I HAVE *the Power* TO MAKE *Change*

30 Day Challenge

This month I will challenge myself by:

1	2	3	4	5	6	7	8	9	10
11	12	13	14	15	16	17	18	19	20
21	22	23	24	25	26	27	28	29	30

My reason why:

Action Steps:

- _____
- _____
- _____
- _____

I will celebrate by:

What is your number 1 goal for this month? Write it in the circle. Brainstorm 4 action steps that will help you towards your goal.

How will achieving this goal improve my life?

What is in my way? How can I make it go away?

ACTION STEPS

1
- _____
- _____
- _____
- _____

2
- _____
- _____
- _____
- _____

3
- _____
- _____
- _____
- _____

4
- _____
- _____
- _____
- _____

Time I am willing to set aside to complete my tasks: _____

Month:

SUNDAY	MONDAY	TUESDAY	WEDNESDAY	THURSDAY	FRIDAY	SATURDAY

GOALS

AFFIRMATION

PRIORITIES

NOTES

APPOINTMENTS	IMPORTANT DATES	BIRTHDAYS	SPECIAL EVENTS
_____	_____	_____	_____
_____	_____	_____	_____
_____	_____	_____	_____
_____	_____	_____	_____
_____	_____	_____	_____

THIS MONTH I WILL EXPAND MY KNOWLEDGE AND LEARN ABOUT

Monthly Book List

BOOK	BOOK	BOOK	BOOK
☆☆☆☆☆ Progress	☆☆☆☆☆ Progress	☆☆☆☆☆ Progress	☆☆☆☆☆ Progress

Identify the habits that you will practice daily to help you achieve your monthly goals.

HABIT TRACKER	1	2	3	4	5	6	7	8	9	10	11	12	13	14	15	16	17	18	19	20	21	22	23	24	25	26	27	28	29	30	31

Week:

MONDAY	TUESDAY	WEDNESDAY

THURSDAY	FRIDAY	SATURDAY

SUNDAY

PASSION. PURPOSE. PROGRESS. NEVER STOP GROWING!

This Week I am Grateful for:

TO DO:

- _____
- _____
- _____
- _____
- _____
- _____

- _____
- _____
- _____
- _____
- _____
- _____

- _____
- _____
- _____
- _____
- _____
- _____

APPOINTMENTS

- _____
- _____
- _____
- _____
- _____
- _____
- _____
- _____

MEALS

M _____
T _____
W _____
TH _____
F _____
S _____
SU _____

SHOPPING LIST

- _____
- _____
- _____
- _____
- _____
- _____
- _____

NOTES

Weekly Reflection

On a scale of 1-10, rate your week. - 1 2 3 4 5 6 7 8 9 10

How am I feeling? Why do I feel this way?

What went well this week? How am I progressing?

This week I learned:

I would like to improve on:

Things I am proud of?

Weekly Reflection

Things I need to let go of?

What habits did I maintain?

What habits were difficult for me to maintain?

How can I make next week better?

What will be realistic targets for next week? Do I need to revise my objectives

Week:

MONDAY	TUESDAY	WEDNESDAY

THURSDAY	FRIDAY	SATURDAY

SUNDAY

PASSION. PURPOSE. PROGRESS. NEVER STOP GROWING!

This Week I am Grateful for:

TO DO:

- _____
- _____
- _____
- _____
- _____
- _____
- _____

- _____
- _____
- _____
- _____
- _____
- _____
- _____

- _____
- _____
- _____
- _____
- _____
- _____
- _____

APPOINTMENTS | MEALS | SHOPPING LIST

- _____
- _____
- _____
- _____
- _____
- _____
- _____
- _____

M _____
T _____
W _____
TH _____
F _____
S _____
SU _____

- _____
- _____
- _____
- _____
- _____
- _____
- _____
- _____

NOTES

Weekly Reflection

On a scale of 1-10, rate your week. - 1 2 3 4 5 6 7 8 9 10

How am I feeling? Why do I feel this way?

What went well this week? How am I progressing?

This week I learned:

I would like to improve on:

Things I am proud of?

Weekly Reflection

Things I need to let go of?

What habits did I maintain?

What habits were difficult for me to maintain?

How can I make next week better?

What will be realistic targets for next week? Do I need to revise my objectives

Week:

MONDAY

TUESDAY

WEDNESDAY

THURSDAY

FRIDAY

SATURDAY

SUNDAY

PASSION. PURPOSE. PROGRESS. NEVER STOP GROWING!

This Week I am Grateful for:

TO DO:

APPOINTMENTS

MEALS

M
T
W
TH
F
S
SU

SHOPPING LIST

NOTES

Weekly Reflection

On a scale of 1-10, rate your week. - 1 2 3 4 5 6 7 8 9 10

How am I feeling? Why do I feel this way?

What went well this week? How am I progressing?

This week I learned:

I would like to improve on:

Things I am proud of?

Weekly Reflection

Things I need to let go of?

What habits did I maintain?

What habits were difficult for me to maintain?

How can I make next week better?

What will be realistic targets for next week? Do I need to revise my objectives

Week:

MONDAY	TUESDAY	WEDNESDAY

THURSDAY	FRIDAY	SATURDAY

SUNDAY

PASSION. PURPOSE. PROGRESS. NEVER STOP GROWING!

This Week I am Grateful for:

TO DO:

APPOINTMENTS

MEALS

M
T
W
TH
F
S
SU

SHOPPING LIST

NOTES

Weekly Reflection

On a scale of 1-10, rate your week. - 1 2 3 4 5 6 7 8 9 10

How am I feeling? Why do I feel this way?

What went well this week? How am I progressing?

This week I learned:

I would like to improve on:

Things I am proud of?

Weekly Reflection

Things I need to let go of?

What habits did I maintain?

What habits were difficult for me to maintain?

How can I make next week better?

**What will be realistic targets for next week?
Do I need to revise my objectives**

Week:

MONDAY

TUESDAY

WEDNESDAY

THURSDAY

FRIDAY

SATURDAY

SUNDAY

PASSION. PURPOSE. PROGRESS. NEVER STOP GROWING!

This Week I am Grateful for:

TO DO:

APPOINTMENTS

MEALS

M
T
W
TH
F
S
SU

SHOPPING LIST

NOTES

Weekly Reflection

On a scale of 1-10, rate your week. - 1 2 3 4 5 6 7 8 9 10

How am I feeling? Why do I feel this way?

What went well this week? How am I progressing?

This week I learned:

I would like to improve on:

Things I am proud of?

Weekly Reflection

Things I need to let go of?

What habits did I maintain?

What habits were difficult for me to maintain?

How can I make next week better?

What will be realistic targets for next week? Do I need to revise my objectives

MY INTENTIONS, *Purpose* AND EFFORTS *are alligned*

Monthly Reflection

What went well this month? How am I progressing?

Did I reach my goal? Why or why not?

How will I rate my efforts this month? How can I get better?

What will be realistic targets for next month? Do I need to revise my objectives?

Free space for notes sketching, mind-mapping and more.

SET A GOAL MAKE A PLAN. YOUR POSSIBILITIES ARE LIMITLESS.

SUCCESS *is a Series* OF SMALL *Wins*

30 Day CHALLENGE

This month I will challenge myself by:

1	2	3	4	5	6	7	8	9	10
11	12	13	14	15	16	17	18	19	20
21	22	23	24	25	26	27	28	29	30

My reason why:

Action Steps:

- _____
- _____
- _____

- _____
- _____
- _____

I will celebrate by:

What is your number 1 goal for this month? Write it in the circle. Brainstorm 4 action steps that will help you towards your goal.

How will achieving this goal improve my life?

What is in my way? How can I make it go away?

ACTION STEPS

1
- _____
- _____
- _____
- _____

2
- _____
- _____
- _____
- _____

3
- _____
- _____
- _____
- _____

4
- _____
- _____
- _____
- _____

Time I am willing to set aside to complete my tasks: _____

Month:

SUNDAY	MONDAY	TUESDAY	WEDNESDAY	THURSDAY	FRIDAY	SATURDAY

GOALS

AFFIRMATION

PRIORITIES

NOTES

APPOINTMENTS	IMPORTANT DATES	BIRTHDAYS	SPECIAL EVENTS
_____	_____	_____	_____
_____	_____	_____	_____
_____	_____	_____	_____
_____	_____	_____	_____
_____	_____	_____	_____

THIS MONTH I WILL EXPAND MY KNOWLEDGE AND LEARN ABOUT

Monthly Book List

BOOK	BOOK	BOOK	BOOK
☆☆☆☆☆ ☐	☆☆☆☆☆ ☐	☆☆☆☆☆ ☐	☆☆☆☆☆ ☐
Progress	Progress	Progress	Progress

Identify the habits that you will practice daily to help you achieve your monthly goals.

HABIT TRACKER	1	2	3	4	5	6	7	8	9	10	11	12	13	14	15	16	17	18	19	20	21	22	23	24	25	26	27	28	29	30	31

Week:

MONDAY

TUESDAY

WEDNESDAY

THURSDAY

FRIDAY

SATURDAY

SUNDAY

PASSION. PURPOSE. PROGRESS. NEVER STOP GROWING!

This Week I am Grateful for:

TO DO:

APPOINTMENTS

MEALS

M
T
W
TH
F
S
SU

SHOPPING LIST

NOTES

Weekly Reflection

On a scale of 1-10, rate your week. - 1 2 3 4 5 6 7 8 9 10

How am I feeling? Why do I feel this way?

What went well this week? How am I progressing?

This week I learned:

I would like to improve on:

Things I am proud of?

Weekly Reflection

Things I need to let go of?

What habits did I maintain?

What habits were difficult for me to maintain?

How can I make next week better?

**What will be realistic targets for next week?
Do I need to revise my objectives**

Week:

MONDAY	TUESDAY	WEDNESDAY

THURSDAY	FRIDAY	SATURDAY

SUNDAY

PASSION. PURPOSE. PROGRESS. NEVER STOP GROWING!

This Week I am Grateful for:

TO DO:

APPOINTMENTS

MEALS

- M
- T
- W
- TH
- F
- S
- SU

SHOPPING LIST

NOTES

Weekly Reflection

On a scale of 1-10, rate your week. - 1 2 3 4 5 6 7 8 9 10

How am I feeling? Why do I feel this way?

What went well this week? How am I progressing?

This week I learned:

I would like to improve on:

Things I am proud of?

Weekly Reflection

Things I need to let go of?

What habits did I maintain?

What habits were difficult for me to maintain?

How can I make next week better?

What will be realistic targets for next week? Do I need to revise my objectives

Week:

MONDAY

TUESDAY

WEDNESDAY

THURSDAY

FRIDAY

SATURDAY

SUNDAY

PASSION. PURPOSE. PROGRESS. NEVER STOP GROWING!

This Week I am Grateful for:

TO DO:

- _____
- _____
- _____
- _____
- _____
- _____
- _____

- _____
- _____
- _____
- _____
- _____
- _____
- _____

- _____
- _____
- _____
- _____
- _____
- _____
- _____

APPOINTMENTS

- _____
- _____
- _____
- _____
- _____
- _____
- _____
- _____

MEALS

M _____
T _____
W _____
TH _____
F _____
S _____
SU _____

SHOPPING LIST

- _____
- _____
- _____
- _____
- _____
- _____
- _____
- _____

NOTES

Weekly Reflection

On a scale of 1-10, rate your week. - 1 2 3 4 5 6 7 8 9 10

How am I feeling? Why do I feel this way?

What went well this week? How am I progressing?

This week I learned:

I would like to improve on:

Things I am proud of?

Weekly Reflection

Things I need to let go of?

What habits did I maintain?

What habits were difficult for me to maintain?

How can I make next week better?

**What will be realistic targets for next week?
Do I need to revise my objectives**

Week:

MONDAY

TUESDAY

WEDNESDAY

THURSDAY

FRIDAY

SATURDAY

SUNDAY

PASSION. PURPOSE. PROGRESS. NEVER STOP GROWING!

This Week I am Grateful for:

TO DO:

- _____
- _____
- _____
- _____
- _____
- _____
- _____

- _____
- _____
- _____
- _____
- _____
- _____
- _____

- _____
- _____
- _____
- _____
- _____
- _____
- _____

APPOINTMENTS

- _____
- _____
- _____
- _____
- _____
- _____
- _____
- _____

MEALS

M _____
T _____
W _____
TH _____
F _____
S _____
SU _____

SHOPPING LIST

- _____
- _____
- _____
- _____
- _____
- _____
- _____
- _____

NOTES

Weekly Reflection

On a scale of 1-10, rate your week. - 1 2 3 4 5 6 7 8 9 10

How am I feeling? Why do I feel this way?

What went well this week? How am I progressing?

This week I learned:

I would like to improve on:

Things I am proud of?

Weekly Reflection

Things I need to let go of?

What habits did I maintain?

What habits were difficult for me to maintain?

How can I make next week better?

What will be realistic targets for next week? Do I need to revise my objectives

Week:

MONDAY

TUESDAY

WEDNESDAY

THURSDAY

FRIDAY

SATURDAY

SUNDAY

PASSION. PURPOSE. PROGRESS. NEVER STOP GROWING!

This Week I am Grateful for:

TO DO:

- _____
- _____
- _____
- _____
- _____
- _____
- _____

- _____
- _____
- _____
- _____
- _____
- _____
- _____

- _____
- _____
- _____
- _____
- _____
- _____
- _____

APPOINTMENTS

- _____
- _____
- _____
- _____
- _____
- _____
- _____
- _____

MEALS

M _____
T _____
W _____
TH _____
F _____
S _____
SU _____

SHOPPING LIST

- _____
- _____
- _____
- _____
- _____
- _____
- _____
- _____

NOTES

Weekly Reflection

On a scale of 1-10, rate your week. - 1 2 3 4 5 6 7 8 9 10

How am I feeling? Why do I feel this way?

What went well this week? How am I progressing?

This week I learned:

I would like to improve on:

Things I am proud of?

Weekly Reflection

Things I need to let go of?

What habits did I maintain?

What habits were difficult for me to maintain?

How can I make next week better?

What will be realistic targets for next week? Do I need to revise my objectives

I WILL CRUSH *My Goals*

Monthly Reflection

What went well this month? How am I progressing?

Did I reach my goal? Why or why not?

How will I rate my efforts this month? How can I get better?

What will be realistic targets for next month? Do I need to revise my objectives?

Free space for notes sketching, mind-mapping and more.

SET A GOAL MAKE A PLAN. YOUR POSSIBILITIES ARE LIMITLESS.

CELEBRATE
Every
TINY
Victory

30 Day CHALLENGE

This month I will challenge myself by:

1	2	3	4	5	6	7	8	9	10
11	12	13	14	15	16	17	18	19	20
21	22	23	24	25	26	27	28	29	30

My reason why:

Action Steps:

- _____
- _____
- _____

- _____
- _____
- _____

I will celebrate by:

What is your number 1 goal for this month? Write it in the circle. Brainstorm 4 action steps that will help you towards your goal.

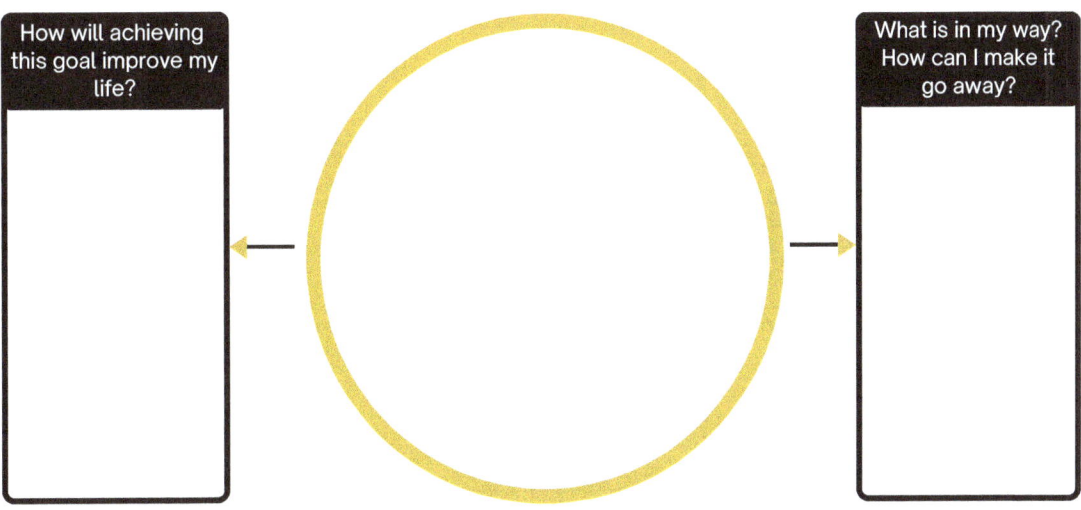

How will achieving this goal improve my life?

What is in my way? How can I make it go away?

ACTION STEPS

1
- _____
- _____
- _____
- _____

2
- _____
- _____
- _____
- _____

3
- _____
- _____
- _____
- _____

4
- _____
- _____
- _____
- _____

Time I am willing to set aside to complete my tasks: _____

Month:

SUNDAY	MONDAY	TUESDAY	WEDNESDAY	THURSDAY	FRIDAY	SATURDAY

GOALS

AFFIRMATION

PRIORITIES

NOTES

APPOINTMENTS	IMPORTANT DATES	BIRTHDAYS	SPECIAL EVENTS
_____	_____	_____	_____
_____	_____	_____	_____
_____	_____	_____	_____
_____	_____	_____	_____
_____	_____	_____	_____

THIS MONTH I WILL EXPAND MY KNOWLEDGE AND LEARN ABOUT

Monthly Book List

BOOK	BOOK	BOOK	BOOK
☆☆☆☆☆ ☐	☆☆☆☆☆ ☐	☆☆☆☆☆ ☐	☆☆☆☆☆ ☐
Progress	Progress	Progress	Progress

Identify the habits that you will practice daily to help you achieve your monthly goals.

HABIT TRACKER	1	2	3	4	5	6	7	8	9	10	11	12	13	14	15	16	17	18	19	20	21	22	23	24	25	26	27	28	29	30	31

Week:

MONDAY

TUESDAY

WEDNESDAY

THURSDAY

FRIDAY

SATURDAY

SUNDAY

PASSION. PURPOSE. PROGRESS. NEVER STOP GROWING!

This Week I am Grateful for:

TO DO:

- _____
- _____
- _____
- _____
- _____
- _____
- _____

- _____
- _____
- _____
- _____
- _____
- _____
- _____

- _____
- _____
- _____
- _____
- _____
- _____
- _____

APPOINTMENTS

- _____
- _____
- _____
- _____
- _____
- _____
- _____
- _____

MEALS

M _____
T _____
W _____
TH _____
F _____
S _____
SU _____

SHOPPING LIST

- _____
- _____
- _____
- _____
- _____
- _____
- _____
- _____

NOTES

Weekly Reflection

On a scale of 1-10, rate your week. - 1 2 3 4 5 6 7 8 9 10

How am I feeling? Why do I feel this way?

What went well this week? How am I progressing?

This week I learned:

I would like to improve on:

Things I am proud of?

Weekly Reflection

Things I need to let go of?

What habits did I maintain?

What habits were difficult for me to maintain?

How can I make next week better?

What will be realistic targets for next week? Do I need to revise my objectives

Week:

MONDAY	TUESDAY	WEDNESDAY

THURSDAY	FRIDAY	SATURDAY

SUNDAY

PASSION. PURPOSE. PROGRESS. NEVER STOP GROWING!

This Week I am Grateful for:

TO DO:

- _____
- _____
- _____
- _____
- _____
- _____
- _____

- _____
- _____
- _____
- _____
- _____
- _____
- _____

- _____
- _____
- _____
- _____
- _____
- _____
- _____

APPOINTMENTS

- _____
- _____
- _____
- _____
- _____
- _____
- _____
- _____

MEALS

M _____
T _____
W _____
TH _____
F _____
S _____
SU _____

SHOPPING LIST

- _____
- _____
- _____
- _____
- _____
- _____
- _____
- _____

NOTES

Weekly Reflection

On a scale of 1-10, rate your week. - 1 2 3 4 5 6 7 8 9 10

How am I feeling? Why do I feel this way?

What went well this week? How am I progressing?

This week I learned:

I would like to improve on:

Things I am proud of?

Weekly Reflection

Things I need to let go of?

What habits did I maintain?

What habits were difficult for me to maintain?

How can I make next week better?

**What will be realistic targets for next week?
Do I need to revise my objectives**

Week:

MONDAY

TUESDAY

WEDNESDAY

THURSDAY

FRIDAY

SATURDAY

SUNDAY

PASSION. PURPOSE. PROGRESS. NEVER STOP GROWING!

This Week I am Grateful for:

TO DO:

- _____
- _____
- _____
- _____
- _____
- _____
- _____

- _____
- _____
- _____
- _____
- _____
- _____

- _____
- _____
- _____
- _____
- _____
- _____
- _____

APPOINTMENTS

- _____
- _____
- _____
- _____
- _____
- _____
- _____
- _____

MEALS

M _____
T _____
W _____
TH _____
F _____
S _____
SU _____

SHOPPING LIST

- _____
- _____
- _____
- _____
- _____
- _____
- _____

NOTES

Weekly Reflection

On a scale of 1-10, rate your week. - 1 2 3 4 5 6 7 8 9 10

How am I feeling? Why do I feel this way?

What went well this week? How am I progressing?

This week I learned:

I would like to improve on:

Things I am proud of?

Weekly Reflection

Things I need to let go of?

What habits did I maintain?

What habits were difficult for me to maintain?

How can I make next week better?

**What will be realistic targets for next week?
Do I need to revise my objectives**

Week:

MONDAY

TUESDAY

WEDNESDAY

THURSDAY

FRIDAY

SATURDAY

SUNDAY

PASSION. PURPOSE. PROGRESS. NEVER STOP GROWING!

This Week I am Grateful for:

TO DO:

APPOINTMENTS

MEALS

M
T
W
TH
F
S
SU

SHOPPING LIST

NOTES

Weekly Reflection

On a scale of 1-10, rate your week. - 1 2 3 4 5 6 7 8 9 10

How am I feeling? Why do I feel this way?

What went well this week? How am I progressing?

This week I learned:

I would like to improve on:

Things I am proud of?

Weekly Reflection

Things I need to let go of?

What habits did I maintain?

What habits were difficult for me to maintain?

How can I make next week better?

What will be realistic targets for next week? Do I need to revise my objectives

Week:

MONDAY

TUESDAY

WEDNESDAY

THURSDAY

FRIDAY

SATURDAY

SUNDAY

PASSION. PURPOSE. PROGRESS. NEVER STOP GROWING!

This Week I am Grateful for:

TO DO:

APPOINTMENTS

MEALS

M
T
W
TH
F
S
SU

SHOPPING LIST

NOTES

Weekly Reflection

On a scale of 1-10, rate your week. - 1 2 3 4 5 6 7 8 9 10

How am I feeling? Why do I feel this way?

What went well this week? How am I progressing?

This week I learned:

I would like to improve on:

Things I am proud of?

Weekly Reflection

Things I need to let go of?

What habits did I maintain?

What habits were difficult for me to maintain?

How can I make next week better?

**What will be realistic targets for next week?
Do I need to revise my objectives**

I ACCOMPLISH *My Goals* DAILY

Monthly Reflection

What went well this month? How am I progressing?

Did I reach my goal? Why or why not?

How will I rate my efforts this month? How can I get better?

What will be realistic targets for next month? Do I need to revise my objectives?

Free space for notes sketching, mind-mapping and more.

SET A GOAL MAKE A PLAN. YOUR POSSIBILITIES ARE LIMITLESS.

START
Somewhere

30 Day CHALLENGE

This month I will challenge myself by:

1	2	3	4	5	6	7	8	9	10
11	12	13	14	15	16	17	18	19	20
21	22	23	24	25	26	27	28	29	30

My reason why:

Action Steps:

- _____
- _____
- _____

- _____
- _____

I will celebrate by:

What is your number 1 goal for this month? Write it in the circle. Brainstorm 4 action steps that will help you towards your goal.

How will achieving this goal improve my life?

What is in my way? How can I make it go away?

ACTION STEPS

1
- _____
- _____
- _____
- _____

2
- _____
- _____
- _____
- _____

3
- _____
- _____
- _____
- _____

4
- _____
- _____
- _____
- _____

Time I am willing to set aside to complete my tasks: _____

Month:

SUNDAY	MONDAY	TUESDAY	WEDNESDAY	THURSDAY	FRIDAY	SATURDAY

GOALS

AFFIRMATION

PRIORITIES

NOTES

APPOINTMENTS	IMPORTANT DATES	BIRTHDAYS	SPECIAL EVENTS
_____	_____	_____	_____
_____	_____	_____	_____
_____	_____	_____	_____
_____	_____	_____	_____
_____	_____	_____	_____

THIS MONTH I WILL EXPAND MY KNOWLEDGE AND LEARN ABOUT

Monthly Book List

BOOK	BOOK	BOOK	BOOK
☆☆☆☆☆ ☐ Progress	☆☆☆☆☆ ☐ Progress	☆☆☆☆☆ ☐ Progress	☆☆☆☆☆ ☐ Progress

Identify the habits that you will practice daily to help you achieve your monthly goals.

HABIT TRACKER	1	2	3	4	5	6	7	8	9	10	11	12	13	14	15	16	17	18	19	20	21	22	23	24	25	26	27	28	29	30	31

Week:

MONDAY

TUESDAY

WEDNESDAY

THURSDAY

FRIDAY

SATURDAY

SUNDAY

PASSION. PURPOSE. PROGRESS. NEVER STOP GROWING!

This Week I am Grateful for:

TO DO:

- _____
- _____
- _____
- _____
- _____
- _____

- _____
- _____
- _____
- _____
- _____
- _____

- _____
- _____
- _____
- _____
- _____
- _____

APPOINTMENTS

- _____
- _____
- _____
- _____
- _____
- _____
- _____

MEALS

M _____
T _____
W _____
TH _____
F _____
S _____
SU _____

SHOPPING LIST

- _____
- _____
- _____
- _____
- _____
- _____
- _____

NOTES

Weekly Reflection

On a scale of 1-10, rate your week. - 1 2 3 4 5 6 7 8 9 10

How am I feeling? Why do I feel this way?

What went well this week? How am I progressing?

This week I learned:

I would like to improve on:

Things I am proud of?

Weekly Reflection

Things I need to let go of?

What habits did I maintain?

What habits were difficult for me to maintain?

How can I make next week better?

What will be realistic targets for next week? Do I need to revise my objectives

Week:

MONDAY

TUESDAY

WEDNESDAY

THURSDAY

FRIDAY

SATURDAY

SUNDAY

PASSION. PURPOSE. PROGRESS. NEVER STOP GROWING!

This Week I am Grateful for:

TO DO:

- _____
- _____
- _____
- _____
- _____
- _____
- _____

- _____
- _____
- _____
- _____
- _____
- _____
- _____

- _____
- _____
- _____
- _____
- _____
- _____
- _____

APPOINTMENTS | MEALS | SHOPPING LIST

- _____
- _____
- _____
- _____
- _____
- _____
- _____
- _____

M _____
T _____
W _____
TH _____
F _____
S _____
SU _____

- _____
- _____
- _____
- _____
- _____
- _____
- _____
- _____

NOTES

Weekly Reflection

On a scale of 1-10, rate your week. - 1 2 3 4 5 6 7 8 9 10

How am I feeling? Why do I feel this way?

What went well this week? How am I progressing?

This week I learned:

I would like to improve on:

Things I am proud of?

Weekly Reflection

Things I need to let go of?

What habits did I maintain?

What habits were difficult for me to maintain?

How can I make next week better?

What will be realistic targets for next week? Do I need to revise my objectives

Week:

MONDAY

TUESDAY

WEDNESDAY

THURSDAY

FRIDAY

SATURDAY

SUNDAY

PASSION. PURPOSE. PROGRESS. NEVER STOP GROWING!

This Week I am Grateful for:

TO DO:

APPOINTMENTS

MEALS

- M
- T
- W
- TH
- F
- S
- SU

SHOPPING LIST

NOTES

Weekly Reflection

On a scale of 1-10, rate your week. - 1 2 3 4 5 6 7 8 9 10

How am I feeling? Why do I feel this way?

What went well this week? How am I progressing?

This week I learned:

I would like to improve on:

Things I am proud of?

Weekly Reflection

Things I need to let go of?

What habits did I maintain?

What habits were difficult for me to maintain?

How can I make next week better?

What will be realistic targets for next week? Do I need to revise my objectives

Week:

MONDAY

TUESDAY

WEDNESDAY

THURSDAY

FRIDAY

SATURDAY

SUNDAY

PASSION. PURPOSE. PROGRESS. NEVER STOP GROWING!

This Week I am Grateful for:

TO DO:

APPOINTMENTS

MEALS

- M
- T
- W
- TH
- F
- S
- SU

SHOPPING LIST

NOTES

Weekly Reflection

On a scale of 1-10, rate your week. - 1 2 3 4 5 6 7 8 9 10

How am I feeling? Why do I feel this way?

What went well this week? How am I progressing?

This week I learned:

I would like to improve on:

Things I am proud of?

Weekly Reflection

Things I need to let go of?

What habits did I maintain?

What habits were difficult for me to maintain?

How can I make next week better?

**What will be realistic targets for next week?
Do I need to revise my objectives**

Week:

MONDAY

TUESDAY

WEDNESDAY

THURSDAY

FRIDAY

SATURDAY

SUNDAY

PASSION. PURPOSE. PROGRESS. NEVER STOP GROWING!

This Week I am Grateful for:

TO DO:

- _____
- _____
- _____
- _____
- _____
- _____
- _____

- _____
- _____
- _____
- _____
- _____
- _____
- _____

- _____
- _____
- _____
- _____
- _____
- _____
- _____

APPOINTMENTS

- _____
- _____
- _____
- _____
- _____
- _____
- _____
- _____

MEALS

M _____
T _____
W _____
TH _____
F _____
S _____
SU _____

SHOPPING LIST

- _____
- _____
- _____
- _____
- _____
- _____
- _____
- _____

NOTES

Weekly Reflection

On a scale of 1-10, rate your week. - 1 2 3 4 5 6 7 8 9 10

How am I feeling? Why do I feel this way?

What went well this week? How am I progressing?

This week I learned:

I would like to improve on:

Things I am proud of?

Weekly Reflection

Things I need to let go of?

What habits did I maintain?

What habits were difficult for me to maintain?

How can I make next week better?

**What will be realistic targets for next week?
Do I need to revise my objectives**

MY DRIVE AND *Ambition* ALLOW ME TO ACHIEVE *My Goals*

Monthly Reflection

What went well this month? How am I progressing?

Did I reach my goal? Why or why not?

How will I rate my efforts this month? How can I get better?

What will be realistic targets for next month? Do I need to revise my objectives?

Free space for notes sketching, mind-mapping and more.

SET A GOAL MAKE A PLAN. YOUR POSSIBILITIES ARE LIMITLESS.

Mind over
MATTER

Yearly Overview

JANUARY	FEBRUARY	MARCH
APRIL	MAY	JUNE
JULY	AUGUST	SEPTEMBER
OCTOBER	NOVEMBER	DECEMBER

BOOKS I WANT *To Read*

Password Tracker

WEBSITE	USERNAME	PASSWORD

Courses I am Taking

Date	Task	✓	Date	Task	✓

Good Things TAKE TIME

Notes

Notes

BE BRAVE, BE FEARLESS, BE YOU! – *Kayla Chew*

WWW.KAYSUPASAIYAN.COM

www.ingramcontent.com/pod-product-compliance
Lightning Source LLC
Chambersburg PA
CBHW080724300426
44114CB00019B/2483